Political
Activists of
the 1960s

By Stuart A. Kallen

LUCENT
BOOKS®

THOMSON
——————✳——————™
GALE

San Diego • Detroit • New York • San Francisco • Cleveland
New Haven, Conn. • Waterville, Maine • London • Munich

THOMSON
GALE

On Cover: (center) Martin Luther King Jr.; (clockwise from top right) Angela Davis, Abbie Hoffman, and Cesar Chavez

LIBRARY OF CONGRESS CATALOGING-IN-PUBLICATION DATA

Kallen, Stuart A., 1955–
    Political activists of the 1960s / Stuart A. Kallen.
        v. cm. — (Lucent history makers series)
    Contents: Martin Luther King Jr.—Dagmar Wilson—Tom Hayden—Cesar Chavez—Betty Friedan—Abbie Hoffman—Angela Davis.
    ISBN 1-59018-386-X (hardcover)
    1. Political activists—United States—Biography—Juvenile literature. 2. Social reformers—United States—Biography—Juvenile literature. 3. United States—History—1961–1969—Juvenile literature. 4. United States—Social conditions—1960–1980—Juvenile literature. [1. Political activists. 2. Reformers. 3. United States—History—1961–1969. 4. United States—Social conditions—1960–1980.] I. Title. II. History makers.
    HN59.K353 2004
    322.4'092'273—dc22

                                                              2003024851

CONTENTS

The literary form most often referred to as "multiple biography" was perfected in the first century A.D. by Plutarch, a perceptive and talented moralist and historian who hailed from the small town of Chaeronea in central Greece. His most famous work, *Parallel Lives*, consists of a long series of biographies of noteworthy ancient Greek and Roman statesmen and military leaders. Frequently, Plutarch compares a famous Greek to a famous Roman, pointing out similarities in personality and achievements. These expertly constructed and very readable tracts provided later historians and others, including playwrights like Shakespeare, with priceless information about prominent ancient personages and also inspired new generations of writers to tackle the multiple biography genre.

The Lucent History Makers series proudly carries on the venerable tradition handed down from Plutarch. Each volume in the series consists of a set of five to eight biographies of important and influential historical figures who were linked together by a common factor. In *Rulers of Ancient Rome*, for example, all the figures were generals, consuls, or emperors of either the Roman Republic or Empire; while the subjects of *Fighters Against American Slavery*, though they lived in different places and times, all shared the same goal, namely, the eradication of human servitude. Mindful that politicians and military leaders are not (and never have been) the only people who shape the course of history, the editors of the series have also included representatives from a wide range of endeavors, including scientists, artists, writers, philosophers, religious leaders, and sports figures.

Each book is intended to give a range of figures—some well known, others less known; some who made a great impact on history, others who made only a small impact. For instance, by making Columbus's initial voyage possible, Spain's Queen Isabella I, featured in *Women Leaders of Nations*, helped to open up the New World to exploration and exploitation by the European powers. Inarguably, therefore, she made a major contribution to a series of events that had momentous consequences for the entire world. By contrast, Catherine II, the eighteenth-century Russian queen, and Golda Meir, the modern Israeli prime minister, did not play roles of global impact; however, their policies and actions significantly influenced the historical development of both their own countries and their regional neighbors. Regardless of their relative importance in the greater historical scheme, all of the figures chronicled in the History Makers series made contributions to posterity; and their public achievements, as well as what is known about their private lives, are presented and evaluated in light of the most recent scholarship.

In addition, each volume in the series is documented and substantiated by a wide array of primary and secondary source quotations. The primary source quotes enliven the text by presenting eyewitness views of the times and culture in which each history maker lived, while the secondary source quotes, taken from the works of respected modern scholars, offer expert elaboration and/ or critical commentary. Each quote is footnoted, demonstrating to the reader exactly where biographers find their information. The footnotes also provide the reader with the means of conducting additional research. Finally, to further guide and illuminate readers, each volume in the series features photographs, two bibliographies, and a comprehensive index.

The History Makers series provides both students engaged in research and more casual readers with informative, enlightening, and entertaining overviews of individuals from a variety of circumstances, professions, and backgrounds. No doubt all of them, whether loved or hated, benevolent or cruel, constructive or destructive, will remain endlessly fascinating to each new generation seeking to identify the forces that shaped their world.

A Politically Charged Era

The sixties are often remembered as a time of sit-ins, protest marches, and calls for revolution. Although a 1964 Gallup Poll found that 75 percent of Americans trusted the federal government to do the right thing and tell them the truth, many citizens were intensely critical of their government. People marched arm-in-arm through the streets of America's cities to protest racial discrimination, war, and sexism.

The Civil Rights Movement

Perhaps the first cause to gain national attention was the civil rights movement. In the Deep South, in states including Alabama, Mississippi, Georgia, South Carolina, and North Carolina, African Americans had long been forced to endure segregated facilities—schools, movie theaters, restaurants, buses, train cars, and public restrooms. And black people, while guaranteed the right to vote by the Constitution, were often denied this right in reality because of hurdles that prevented them from registering to vote.

Beginning in the 1950s and throughout the 1960s, political activists pursued a variety of methods to end these practices. People conducted nonviolent demonstrations called sit-ins in which protesters sat down in a public place and refused to move, often to the point that police would physically remove and arrest them. They led registration drives encouraging African Americans to sign up to vote. At seminars called teach-ins, activists taught young African Americans black history and culture. Large demonstrations were utilized in major cities, such as Washington, D.C., as a means of drawing widespread media attention to the cause. Organizations such as the Southern Christian Leadership Conference, brought lawsuits in state and federal courts to overturn segregationist laws.

These methods were helpful in ending segregation in the South during the sixties. Some African Americans in the North, however, particularly in the cities, did not think nonviolent protest was going to help them, since largely white political machines and police forces enforced widespread, if informal, discrimination. Groups such as the Black Panthers advocated revolution and the violent overthrow of the white power structure. They often sought black autonomy and self-sufficiency instead of integration. Toward this end they set up free breakfast programs, medical clinics, and legal services for inner-city residents.

The Antiwar Cause

Some of the protest techniques developed by the civil rights activists provided inspiration to those who came to oppose the Vietnam War. Beginning in 1965, antiwar activists utilized sit-ins, teach-ins, and mass demonstrations to express opposition to the war. Others, following the lead of the Black Panthers, called for the complete restructuring of society. They wanted to take power away from corporations and wealthy individuals, whom they blamed for promoting the war. While their philosophies echoed Socialist dogma despised by many in the United States, their methods of publicizing their message were decidedly American. Groups such as the Yippies were skilled in staging outrageous stunts in order to get attention in the national news media.

In 1965 Martin Luther King Jr. (front, center) led a protest in Montgomery, Alabama, against state-imposed restrictions on the right of blacks to register for the vote.

Equal Pay and Equal Rights

Feminists were similarly inspired by the actions of the civil rights movement. By the late sixties, women saw an opportunity to right long-standing inequities. They sought to pass laws that guaranteed women rights and pay equal to that of men. Several dozen women founded the National Organization for Women (NOW), which became extremely influential in shaping government policies regarding women's rights.

In California, meanwhile, labor organizers were concerned with gaining protections for Hispanic farmworkers, who were treated as virtual slaves by large agribusiness companies. By using nonviolent methods similar to those employed by civil rights activists, these labor organizers were able to improve the lot of farmworkers.

Ahead of Their Time

While many Americans demonstrated for political and social change, a few walked at the very front of the march. Following deeply held beliefs, these political activists put themselves at risk. For their often unpopular positions they received countless death threats. They were sometimes arrested. And in some cases FBI agents read their mail, tapped their phones, and followed them everywhere they went.

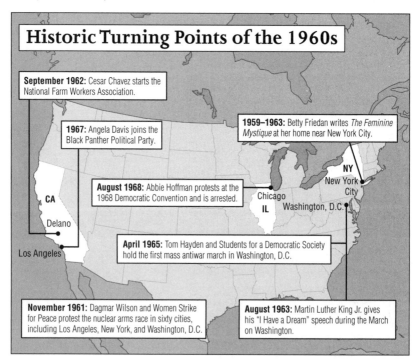

Historic Turning Points of the 1960s

September 1962: Cesar Chavez starts the National Farm Workers Association.

1967: Angela Davis joins the Black Panther Political Party.

1959–1963: Betty Friedan writes *The Feminine Mystique* at her home near New York City.

August 1968: Abbie Hoffman protests at the 1968 Democratic Convention and is arrested.

April 1965: Tom Hayden and Students for a Democratic Society hold the first mass antiwar march in Washington, D.C.

November 1961: Dagmar Wilson and Women Strike for Peace protest the nuclear arms race in sixty cities, including Los Angeles, New York, and Washington, D.C.

August 1963: Martin Luther King Jr. gives his "I Have a Dream" speech during the March on Washington.

NY
New York City
CA
Delano
Los Angeles
Chicago
IL
Washington, D.C.

In many ways, the political activists of the 1960s were ahead of their time. When they first began organizing protests and strikes, many people, even those who supported their beliefs, thought they were fighting for lost causes. No one, for example, had ever successfully organized hundreds of thousands of people to protest against their country going to war. Those in the civil rights movement were fighting centuries of tradition that made discrimination accepted throughout most of society.

Today few question the rightness of what these activists fought for. Gender and racial discrimination have been banned by law in the United States and are widely seen as having been wrong. While protests against war are somtimes controversial, millions now regard the Vietnam War as having been a terrible mistake—if not outright immoral. Moreover, advocates of peace today employ tactics popularized by sixties organizers. While war, racism, and discrimination might never be eliminated, the dreams of political activists from the 1960s have become reality, not just in America, but in many places throughout the world today.

CHAPTER 1

Martin Luther King Jr.

Martin Luther King Jr. is perhaps the most revered of those who fought for civil rights. His name is familiar to almost everyone, and his success in ending government-sanctioned segregation has vastly improved the lives of tens of millions of people of all races.

King was born in Atlanta, Georgia, on January 15, 1929, into a world of prejudice and discrimination. At that time, African Americans were living under a policy of legal segregation known as "Jim Crow." More than thirty years earlier, the Supreme Court had ruled that black people could be kept separated from whites in schools and in other places as long as the facilities were equal in quality. Black people were indeed separated from whites, but in practice there was no equality. For example, in the South, states spent an average of ten times more money on schools for whites as they did on black schools. Most black children attended schools in run-down buildings with few books or supplies.

Despite Jim Crow, little Martin and his family lived better than most blacks in the American South. His parents owned their twelve-room home on tree-lined Auburn Avenue. The neighborhood, although segregated, was prosperous, being home to many of Atlanta's black doctors, lawyers, and businesspeople.

Family Life

Martin was the first child born to Alberta Williams King and Martin Luther King Sr. Everyone called the young Martin "M.L." to distinguish him from his father, who was known as "Daddy King." King Sr. was the highly respected pastor at the Ebenezer Baptist Church, also located on Auburn Avenue.

Daddy King was a large, strong man with a dynamic personality. By the time M.L. was born, Daddy King was a powerful leader in the black community. In addition to being a preacher, he was an executive director of the Atlanta NAACP (National Association for the Advancement of Colored People), the most prominent civil rights organization in the country at that time.

M.L. grew up in the Ebenezer Baptist Church, and this world of religion and celebration structured his life. Historian Stephen B.

Oates in *Let the Trumpet Sound: The Life of Martin Luther King, Jr.* notes:

> The church was M.L.'s second home. All his close friends were in his Sunday-school classes. . . . After Sunday school came regular worship in the sanctuary, a voltage-charged affair in which the congregation swayed and cried . . . as Reverend King preached in remarkable oratorical nourishes, his voice ranging from a booming baritone to a near shriek. . . .
>
> After worship came Sunday dinner at church—succulent fried chicken, ham, black-eyed peas, and watermelon—and then more devotionals and religious activities that lasted into the night. . . . The church defined his little-boy world, gave it order and balance, taught him how to get along with people. Here M.L. knew who he was—"Reverend King's boy," somebody special.[1]

Facing Discrimination

Despite his family's prominence, M.L. was not immune to the racism common at the time. His first experience with discrimination came when he was only six years old. At that time, M.L. had a white playmate named Billy, the son of a local shopkeeper. The

Martin Luther King Jr. was the first child born to Martin Luther King Sr. (left), a respected Baptist minister, and Alberta Williams King (second from left).

boys had been friends since they were toddlers. When they reached school age, however, Billy shocked M.L., saying that his father had forbade him to play with Martin anymore because he was black. At the dinner table that night, M.L. asked his parents the reason for Billy's new attitude. For the first time, M.L. was told of the racist treatment that many white people directed against African Americans. Martin's parents also told him of their own experiences with discrimination and humiliation. M.L.'s parents told him it was his Christian duty, however, to love everyone, even whites who mistreated him, and this puzzled him. He would later recall: "The question arose in my mind: How could I love a race of people who hated me and who had been responsible for breaking me up with one of my best childhood friends? This was a great question in my mind for a number of years."[2]

M.L. faced other problems as well. Daddy King had a fierce and violent temper and would often dole out painful whippings to M.L. even when he was a teenager. M.L. responded to this abuse with a determination to oppose violence in any form.

Higher Education

M.L. was an intelligent child and an excellent student, so much so that he was able to skip two grades in high school. He was, therefore, only fifteen when he enrolled in Morehouse College in 1944. To earn extra money for college, young King joined a work program that took him to Hartford, Connecticut. This experience changed the young man's life. While there was still obvious prejudice directed at black people in Hartford, it was an integrated city. This meant that King and his friends could eat in any restaurant, sit anywhere on the bus, and choose any seat they wanted in any movie theater. King vowed that he would one day work to rid the South of segregation.

While at Morehouse, King decided he wanted to become a minister. To further that goal, after graduation he attended the Crozer Theological Seminary in Chester, Pennsylvania. It was while studying at Crozer that King discovered the works of Mohandas Gandhi, who had led a movement that had recently ended more than 170 years of British colonial rule in India. Gandhi had succeeded by embracing nonviolent resistance and by preaching love for his enemies. He organized boycotts and strikes, and when British soldiers retaliated with vicious beatings, his followers simply lay down in the streets. Gandhi's story made a powerful impression on the young would-be minister. As Oates writes, King believed that "Ghandi's was the only moral and practical way for

As a university student, King decided to become a minister. In 1955 he became head minister at the Dexter Avenue Baptist Church in Montgomery, Alabama.

oppressed [African Americans] to struggle against social injustice."[3]

In 1951 King received his undergraduate degree from Crozer. Deciding to pursue advance studies, that fall he enrolled in Boston University's School of Theology. It was while studying in Boston that King met Coretta Scott. The couple went on a date, and King told her right away that she was everything he was looking for in a wife. Although Scott, a Methodist, was reluctant to marry a Baptist minister, the couple was engaged within six months. They were married in 1953.

Meanwhile, King had continued his graduate studies and in 1955 received his doctorate. Even before he was officially granted his degree, King took a job as head minister at the Dexter Avenue Church in Montgomery, Alabama. Now King would have a chance to fight racism in one of the bastions of segregation.

Equal Rights on the Bus

That chance came before the end of his first year in Montgomery. On December 1, 1955, Rosa Parks, a tailor's assistant at a Montgomery department store, was riding a bus home from work. She had found an empty seat in the section of the bus reserved for blacks. After a few minutes, however, several white passengers boarded, taking the last seats in the whites-only section. A white man, who had been left standing, demanded that Parks give up her seat. She refused, and within minutes police arrived, dragged her off the bus, and took her to jail.

The next morning E.D. Nixon, leader of the Montgomery chapter of the NAACP, called King and told him of the arrest of Rosa Parks. Nixon was hoping to use the Parks case to galvanize public support for a boycott that would pressure authorities to end segregation in public transportation. Such an action stood a chance of working: A boycott would cost the bus company a lot of money since there were forty thousand black riders compared to only twelve thousand white riders.

King agreed to help by holding a meeting at his church, to be attended by other pastors of black churches in Montgomery. Forty-five ministers showed up and agreed to urge their parishioners to support the boycott. Thirty-five thousand flyers were printed up to inform people of the plan. A group called the Montgomery Improvement Association (MIA), was formed to coordinate boycott activities. King was elected president.

December 5, 1955, was the first day of the Montgomery bus boycott, and that morning, the buses were empty. People walked,

In 1955 Rosa Parks (being interviewed) was arrested for refusing to give up her seat on a Montgomery bus to a white man. In response, King organized a boycott of the city's bus system.

hitchhiked, and even rode mules and horses to work. In addition, sixty African American cab drivers volunteered to provide rides for only ten cents—the fare bus riders paid.

That night, King decided to give a speech to draw attention to the boycott. Speaking without notes, King addressed a crowd of over four thousand people, including reporters from the national media, saying, "There comes a time when people get tired. We are here this evening to say to those who have mistreated us for so long that we are tired—tired of being segregated and humiliated, tired of being kicked about by the brutal feet of oppression." [4] King also asked people to act peacefully and responsibly and to respond to hatred with love.

As one of the boycott's organizers, King became the focus of hatred by whites. At home he was receiving over thirty death threats a day. Hate letters arrived by mail, and vicious and obscene telephone calls came at all hours of the day and night. The threat of violence turned to reality on January 30, 1956, when someone firebombed the Kings' home. Fortunately for King, who was not home at the time, Coretta, and their young daughter, Yolanda, escaped unharmed. Some in a crowd of angry blacks who gathered at King's house advocated a violent response to the firebomb. King, however, called on the crowd to respond with nonviolence and love. This, according to King's biographer Lerone Bennett Jr., "changed the course of the protest and made King a living symbol. . . . *[Seeing] the idea* of [nonviolence] in action, . . . millions were touched, if not converted."[5]

Despite incidents such as the bombing, the bus boycott lasted throughout most of 1956. During this time, lawyers for the NAACP and the MIA challenged Montgomery's segregationist laws in court. Nearly a year after the boycott began, on November 13, the United States Supreme Court ruled that segregated buses were unconstitutional. The decision took effect on December 20, and King, Nixon, and other black leaders were the first to ride on an integrated bus.

The Southern Christian Leadership Conference

King's leadership and policy of nonviolence during the boycott made him a national figure. His photo appeared on the cover of *Time* magazine, and he was featured in newspaper articles nationwide. That prominence helped King draw national attention to the racist policies that had been in place in the Deep South for sixty years.

For his part, King knew the fight against segregation was not over. He believed that for blacks to achieve lasting progress they would have to keep the pressure on. To coordinate protest activities, King formed the Southern Christian Leadership Conference (SCLC) in January 1957. The organization, with headquarters in Atlanta, consisted of black ministers throughout the South.

King was elected president of the SCLC. Determined to devote his full attention to civil rights, King resigned as head minister at the Dexter Avenue Baptist Church and moved with his family back to Atlanta.

Over the next several years, King organized demonstrations throughout the South. Emulating Gandhi, King and the SCLC staged nonviolent sit-ins and protest marches.

In 1963 King decided to take on his most difficult task to date—ending segregation in Birmingham, Alabama. However, looking toward a broader goal, King hoped the protests in Birmingham would push President John F. Kennedy and the U.S. Congress to pass a federal civil rights bill.

King knew that the authorities would respond violently to protests. The head of the police force in Birmingham was a racist named Eugene "Bull" Connor, and King expected Connor to order the use of tear gas, billy clubs, and attack dogs against the protesters. Such tactics could spark a violent response, so King put protesters through intense training to avoid this. Recruits were taught to resist the urge to fight back, despite being cursed, spit upon, pushed, and even beaten.

On April 4, 1963, the protests began as activists conducted sit-ins at segregated lunch counters. When these people were arrested, more came in to replace them. At the same time, a larger group marched on city hall, singing gospel songs and carrying signs demanding equal rights. These people were also arrested.

The demonstrations continued for more than a week. On April 16, King himself was arrested when he marched to city hall with a small group of protesters. While he sat in his cell, King wrote an open letter to Americans in which he pointed out that African Americans had been waiting 340 years for justice and that many had reached the breaking point: "The Negro has many pent-up resentments and latent frustrations, and he must release them. . . . If repressed emotions are not released in nonviolent ways, they will seek expression through violence; this is not a threat but a fact of history."[6]

The letter was smuggled out of the jail by one of King's lawyers. Over a million copies were made and distributed to churches, newspapers, and politicians.

By the time King was released eleven days later, the protests had come to a standstill—nearly everyone was in jail. Someone suggested involving young people in the protests. King worried about the safety of children who would be subjected to violence but knew that they were directly affected by racism.

On May 2, 1963, one thousand young people marched through Birmingham singing and clapping hands. Police arrested 950 but, the next day another thousand youngsters marched. Now Connor ordered fire hoses turned on the protesters. The water jets were so powerful they ripped clothes from bodies, threw people into the air, and slammed them against buildings. In addition, police used dogs, clubs, and tear gas against the young protesters.

News footage of the vicious attacks on the youths, some as young as six years old, was broadcast that night on TV programs throughout the United States. President Kennedy said he was sickened by what he saw. Meanwhile, powerful Birmingham citizens felt that Connor's actions were becoming a national embarrassment. They decided to sit down with King and negotiate an end to segregation. Nonviolence had won the day.

The March on Washington

What the SCLC called the Children's Crusade had an impact that was felt far beyond Birmingham. On June 11, President Kennedy gave a televised speech in which he announced that he was prepared to introduce a civil rights bill to Congress. King decided to organize a march on Washington, D.C., hoping that this show of black unity would inspire Congress to support the president's initiative.

King expected about one hundred thousand people, while the press said only twenty-five thousand would attend. On the hot, humid morning of August 28, 1963, however, over two hundred fifty thousand people, both black and white, gathered around the Reflecting Pool in front of the Lincoln Memorial in Washington, D.C. The march was part picnic and part politics. People cooled their feet in the pool as gospel and folksingers electrified the crowd. At 3 P.M., King rose to the podium and spoke movingly of

Over 250,000 people listened as King delivered his famous "I Have a Dream" speech at the March on Washington in 1963.

his dream of a day when black and white children would not be segregated and when people would be judged according to their moral stature rather than according to their race.

"Man of the Year"

King's eloquence made him a deeply respected figure internationally. His accomplishments were recognized in 1964 when *Time* magazine made him "Man of the Year." He was the first African American to be so honored. A far greater honor came in December, when King was awarded the prestigious Nobel Peace Prize. In his acceptance speech, he said he was accepting it for all of the 22 million African Americans living in the United States. Meanwhile, the Civil Rights Act was approved by Congress and signed by the new president, Lyndon Johnson. This act banned discrimination on the basis of race, religion, or gender.

Despite his success, King refused to rest. In March 1965 the SCLC organized a four-day, fifty-mile march from Selma, Alabama, to Montgomery to demonstrate in favor of voting rights. At first, the demonstration was declared illegal because the marchers did not have a permit. State troopers tried to break up the march by using tear gas and billy clubs against the demonstrators. King then went to a judge and was granted legal approval for the march. On March 26, over twenty-five thousand people, including national politicians and celebrities, marched on Montgomery. Many observers credit the Selma-to-Montgomery march with forcing Congress to take action. Less than six months later, on August 6, President Johnson signed the Voting Rights Act that required, among other provisions, federal officials to oversee elections to assure fairness.

Cut Down

With voting rights secured and segregation legally banned, King focused his efforts on the disparity in wages between black and white workers. In Memphis, Tennessee, for example, black trash collectors were paid less than their white counterparts. When African American sanitation workers held a strike in protest in April 1968, King traveled to Memphis to help them obtain better wages. On April 4, 1968, at 7 P.M., King was planning a march with the trash collectors. He stepped out on the balcony of his motel to get some air. A shot rang out, and King dropped to the ground, felled by an assassin's bullet. He was just thirty-nine. Millions of Americans were shocked and saddened by King's death. Over one hundred thousand people gathered at the Ebenezer Baptist

King's parents and his wife Coretta attend a memorial service for the slain civil rights leader. King was assassinated in Memphis, Tennessee, on April 4, 1968.

Church for the civil rights leader's funeral. Over 120 million people watched the procession on TV.

After his death, Coretta Scott King established the King Center in Atlanta. The center is a living memorial dedicated to advancing King's message of nonviolence, justice, equality, and peace. In 1983 Congress made King's birthday a national holiday. For twelve years in the fifties and sixties, King selflessly worked to improve the lives of millions of people. He provided vital leadership during a critical time. King's message of peace and nonviolent change has been an inspiration to countless people in the years since he died. Martin Luther King Jr.'s dream has come true for millions of people all over the world.

CHAPTER 2

Dagmar Wilson

The sixties are often remembered for massive demonstrations against the Vietnam War. Even before that war grew into a major conflict, however, thousands of women staged protests against America's military policies. Prominent among these women was Dagmar Searchinger Wilson, a forty-five-year-old mother of three, and a successful illustrator of children's books. Concerned about the threat posed to children's health by nuclear testing, Wilson formed an organization called Women Strike for Peace. Wilson's was one of the first voices raised to ask the world's leaders to end a headlong race toward nuclear annihilation.

Raised in a Political Household

Born in New York City on January 25, 1916, Dagmar was exposed to the world of politics at a very early age. Her father, Caesar Searchinger, took his family to Europe when Dagmar was only three. Searchinger was the European director of the CBS radio broadcasting network, and later became a news analyst for NBC. Dagmar was raised and educated in England and spent hours listening to her father discuss politics with his colleagues, who were also respected news commentators, journalists, and analysts.

For all her father's political awareness, Dagmar later recalled that his was a passive role. The years when Dagmar was growing up were the years in which Nazi leader Adolf Hitler, using violence against his opposition and preaching hatred against Jews and other minority groups, was gaining power in Germany. In a 1976 interview she stated that she felt that her parents could have done more to oppose Hitler. While they wrote and talked endlessly about events, she said, "They did precious little to influence their course."[7]

Meanwhile, the young woman was developing talent as an artist. Between 1933 and 1937 she attended the Slade School of Art in London. After graduation, Searchinger taught art at an elementary school. It was there that she met Christopher Wilson, who also was a teacher. In 1939 the couple moved to the United States, where they were married.

21

A group of female protesters demonstrates against the Vietnam War in Washington, D.C. Throughout the 1960s, women across the country protested America's military policies.

In 1942, the Wilsons moved to Washington, D.C., where Dagmar found work as a graphic artist. By this time the Wilsons had several children, and in 1945 Wilson quit her job in order to be a full-time mother. She continued to paint and exhibit her work at art galleries on occasion, however. In 1946 she illustrated a children's book titled *While Suzie Sleeps*. The book became a bestseller, firmly establishing Wilson in her craft. Over the next fifteen years, Wilson illustrated more than twenty other books.

Getting Involved

Although she was not involved with any political cause, Wilson was growing increasingly anxious about world events. Like so many of her generation, she had witnessed the destruction of World War II. Now, in the late 1950s, the United States and the Soviet Union were engaged in a tense political and military stand-off known as the Cold War. The tension between the United States and the Soviet Union was exacerbated as both sides spent enormous sums building and testing nuclear weapons. These weapons were mounted on missiles and carried aboard bombers. They targeted nearly every large city in Europe and the United States.

Several prominent figures—some whose work had been key to developing nuclear weapons—opposed the escalating arms race. Physicist Albert Einstein, for example, whose theories had made it possible for others to build nuclear weapons, stated that the Cold War

> conflict that exists today is no more than the old-style struggle for power. . . . The difference is that this time the development of atomic power has imbued the struggle with a ghostly character; for [the United States and the

President Kennedy consults with an adviser during a test launch of a nuclear missile. Dagmar Wilson organized the Women Strike for Peace (WSP) to protest the use of such weapons.

Soviet Union] know and admit that should the quarrel deteriorate into actual war, mankind is doomed.[8]

Hearing such statements gave Wilson a sense of foreboding that she could not ignore. She joined what at the time was the leading antinuclear organization, the Committee for a Sane Nuclear Policy, called SANE, eventually becoming the secretary of her local chapter. Wilson quickly became disillusioned with SANE, however, because its leaders most often tried to work by influencing Congress, even when the lawmakers were hostile to the group's agenda.

Moved to Organize

Wilson reached out to other women she had met through SANE who felt similarly. She invited five other women from the Washington, D.C., area to join her in organizing a large-scale protest to call attention to the nuclear arms race. The Women Strike for Peace (WSP) organization was born.

Meanwhile, it looked as though America's leaders were preparing for war. For example, President Kennedy asked Congress to appropriate an emergency $207 million in order to accelerate the building of nuclear fallout shelters in the basements of public buildings. Kennedy also tripled the number of men to be drafted into the military, mobilized reservists, and ordered four hundred thousand military troops to bases in Western Europe.

Tensions rose further still when Soviet premier Nikita Khrushchev announced that the USSR would resume nuclear testing in reaction to the Western troops poised on the border with East Germany. Both the United States and the USSR had agreed in 1958 to a temporary halt to open-air testing of hydrogen bombs, but now Kennedy countered Khrushchev's move by ordering an increase in underground testing with a promise for an atmospheric test to follow. Each side began to accuse the other of breaking the moratorium on testing. In this climate of fear, Wilson called a meeting of the WSP. She later recalled the emotional energy that flowed from a sense that men were putting the world at risk for no good reason:

> It was a warm September night in 1961. Six women sat in a Georgetown living room. We were worried. We were indignant. We were angry. The Soviet Union and the U.S.A. were accusing each other of having broken a moratorium on nuclear testing. What matter who broke it when everyone's children would fall victim to radioactive Strontium

90 [released by the tests]? . . . Perhaps, we told ourselves that night, in the face of male "logic," which seemed to us utterly illogical, it was time for women to speak out.[9]

Women Strike for Peace

Although the WSP was loosely organized, had a small budget, and had no office, the organization picked November 1, 1961, as the day to strike. To publicize the strike, the WSP issued a call for women across the country to "Appeal to All Governments to End the Arms Race—Not the Human Race." Women were asked to walk out of their kitchens and off their jobs. WSP's message was clear: "We strike against death, desolation, destruction and on behalf of liberty and life. . . . Husbands and babysitters take over the home front. Bosses and substitutes take over our jobs!"[10] The message was circulated in phone calls, printed on flyers that were passed out at churches, announced at PTA meetings, and distributed to other peace organizations.

As planned, on November 1, an estimated fifty thousand women protested in sixty American cities including Los Angeles, New York, and Washington, D.C. They carried signs that said, "Save the Children," "[Nuclear] Testing Damages the Unborn," and "Let's Live in Peace Not Pieces."[11] The WSP also appealed to women who were married to powerful men: The group sent letters to the Soviet premier's wife, Nina Khrushchev, and John F. Kennedy's wife, Jacqueline, asking them to talk to their husbands about signing a nuclear test ban treaty. In *Women Strike for Peace*, founding member Amy Swerdlow describes the impact made by the women:

> The women's strike for peace was an instant success in that it drew attention to women's profound fear of the dangers posed to health and life by nuclear testing, and at the same time restored women's voice to foreign policy discourse for the first time since the [end of World War II]. The size of the turnout, its national scope, the traditional and respectable . . . image projected by the women astonished government officials as well as the media. Sophia Wyatt, from London, who marched with the Los Angeles women, tried to determine who and what had brought them out. She asked a woman walking beside her what organization she belonged to. Wyatt reported . . . that the Los Angeles woman replied with a laugh, "I don't belong to any organization. I've got a child of ten."[12]

"A Hue and Cry"

With the publicity garnered by the initial strike, the membership rolls of the WSP swelled as women from across the country—and around the world—joined the group. In the aftermath of WSP's huge success, Wilson worked with other founding members of the WSP to guide the ever-expanding movement.

As the WSP grew in importance, Wilson was a reluctant leader. She did not want to start a bureaucratic organization that depended on one charismatic leader to act as spokesperson. Instead Wilson sat on a steering committee that simply called on local, grassroots WSP chapters to designate the first day of every month as "women strike for peace day." Members of each chapter could visit local politicians, hold rallies, contact the media, and gain attention for the cause in the manner best suited to them and the region where they lived.

Although the group was composed of mothers and housewives, and its members also led such all-American organizations as the Girls Scouts and the PTA, the WSP was quickly accused by politicians and some in the press of harboring Communist sympathies and helping the Soviet Union. Wilson dismissed such accusations

Wilson (fourth from left) marches past the Lincoln Memorial in Washington, D.C., during an anti–Vietnam War demonstration in 1967.

26

Wilson (left) and Coretta Scott King (right) demonstrate in New York against nuclear weapons development. Women from all over the world participated in the WSP's protests.

out of hand, stressing that her complaint was not based on politics but on the differing views held by men and women. She stated:

> You know how men are. They talk in abstractions and prestige and technicalities of the [hydrogen] bomb, almost as if it were all a game of chess. Well, it isn't. There are times, it seems to me, when the only thing to do is let out a loud scream. . . . Just women raising a hue and cry against nuclear weapons for all of them to cut it out.[13]

"The Preservation of Our Families"

By the end of 1962, the WSP had drawn the attention of a powerful Congressional body known as the House Un-American Activities Committee (HUAC). HUAC had been formed in the late 1930s to investigate Communist influence within the United States. Over the years, the committee's members had investigated hundreds of Americans for supposed Communist sympathies. Some of those who refused to cooperate with the committee lost their jobs, faced financial ruin, and were even jailed. Wilson and eight other WSP members were called to testify.

Even before HUAC publicly announced the inquiry, Wilson issued a statement to the *New York Times* saying: "We recognize this investigation as an attempt to divert our attention from the most important issue women have ever faced, the preservation of our families in a world armed with nuclear bombs." She went on to say that Communists were not giving them orders. "We decide everything by group decision, nothing is dictated."[14]

A '"Baffled Congress"

The HUAC hearings commenced on December 11, 1962, in the Caucus Room of the Old House Office Building of the U.S. Congress. That day, the five hundred seats in the Caucus Room were packed with young mothers wearing white gloves and stylish hats. Many were holding infants—and many of the babies were crying. The WSP took control of the hearings immediately. Whenever a WSP member finished testifying, women in the audience would present her with flowers and a standing ovation.

Wilson was scheduled to testify on the third day of the hearings, on December 13. That morning, the women in the Caucus Room all wore white roses tied with ribbons that said, "Women Strike for Peace." When Wilson was called to testify, a loud cheer rocked the room. A young woman holding a baby then stepped forward and presented Wilson with a bouquet of white roses.

The committee members were respectful of Wilson. Their tactic was to prove that she was being naive in failing to understand how her outspoken opinions were aiding the enemy. Wilson responded to such condescension with honesty, humor, and occasional condescension of her own. For example, when asked if she had organized the November 1961 strike in fifty-eight cities she answered: "I find it very hard to explain to the masculine mind. I can't answer yes or no. It was my initiative that resulted in, yes, all of these demonstrations that took place on that day. By the way there were 60, not just 58." When the chairman asked Wilson if she would allow Communists to join her organization, she replied: "Well, my dear sir, I have absolutely no way of controlling . . . who wishes to join the demonstrations. . . . I would like to say that unless everybody in the whole world joins us in this fight, then God help us."[15]

Never before had anyone responded to HUAC in quite the way Wilson and her fellow WSP members had done. Newspapers ridiculed the politicians with headlines like "Peace Gals Make Red Hunters Look Silly," "Redhunters Decapitated," "Peace Ladies Tangle with Baffled Congress," and "It's Ladies Day at Capitol: Hoots, Howls, and Charm."[16] *New York Times* reporter Russell Baker wrote that the Congressmen

> spent most of the [time] looking lonely, badgered, and miserable, less like dashing Red-hunters than like men trapped in a bargain basement on sale day. . . . The . . . luckless politicians watched the procession of gardenias, carnations, and roses with the resigned look of men aware

that they were liable to charges of being against house-wives, children, and peace. . . .[17]

Such negative publicity soon forced HUAC to drop the matter. Seven months after the HUAC hearings, the efforts of the WSP came to fruition. On July 26, 1963, President Kennedy and Premier Khrushchev signed the Partial Nuclear Test Ban Treaty, banning aboveground testing of nuclear weapons. Kennedy acknowledged the role that the WSP had played in pushing him to negotiate the treaty, saying, "I get their message."[18] In addition, Kennedy's science adviser Jerome Weisner credited the WSP and several other peace groups for persuading the president to agree to the ban on aboveground nuclear testing.

Stepping Away from WSP

Although Wilson had triumphed, by the time the test ban treaty was signed, she was rapidly concluding that it was time to part

Wilson (front, left) and members of the WSP prepare to embark on a humanitarian mission in Russia. Some members of the press accused the organization of harboring Communist sympathies.

with the WSP. Not only was her career as an illustrator on hold, but her living room had essentially been taken over by the organization. Leading the WSP had become a full-time job, but paid nothing. Although Wilson hoped that the WSP would provide her with funds to compensate her for her work, none were forthcoming. With a heavy heart, she returned to her career and distanced herself from the WSP. Meanwhile, Women Strike for Peace became one of the first groups to warn against U.S. military involvement in Vietnam, and the group would strenuously oppose the war throughout the 1960s. Wilson, however, only returned to speak at special events and anniversaries.

Throughout the rest of the twentieth century, Wilson worked at the local level as a community activist concentrating on environmental issues, particularly the negative effects of pollution on children. But even after more than three decades of political activism, Wilson felt that there was still work to be done. In 1996, on the thirty-fifth anniversary of the founding of the WSP, Wilson spoke out for a total ban on nuclear testing, which is still conducted underground. She also asked for a halt in the production of nuclear weapons, saying:

> Since we came into being 35 years ago as a protest against atmospheric nuclear tests and the danger of radioactive pollution to children's health, WSP has remained a strong voice in the struggle for our unfinished goal—the Comprehensive Test Ban Treaty and for total nuclear disarmament. . . . As we celebrate our 35th anniversary, we call on women to recommit themselves to the total elimination of nuclear weapons and removing the nuclear threat from future generations.[19]

Always the eloquent spokesperson, Dagmar Searchinger Wilson used intelligence, wit, and compassion to save children from radioactive poisons. In doing so, she helped the world take one small step back from the brink of nuclear annihilation.

CHAPTER 3

Tom Hayden

Tom Hayden in many ways is typical of sixties political activists. He entered college in the late 1950s as a clean-cut student. He was energized in early 1960 by the civil rights movement. In the midsixties he came to oppose the Vietnam War. Not only did his political activities earn him celebrity, they earned him criminal indictment and jail time.

Thomas Emmett Hayden was born on December 11, 1939, in a suburb of Detroit, the son of Irish Americans. The Haydens sent their son to a Catholic school, where he acquired values typical of those expressed in his senior class motto: "To do more for the world than the world does for you, that is success."[20] Despite the idealism contained in such sentiments, like many youngsters growing up in the 1950s, Tom had little interest in politics.

Reporting on Injustice

Hayden graduated from high school with good grades in June 1957, enabling him to enter the University of Michigan at Ann Arbor that fall. Hoping to pursue a career in writing, Hayden was attracted to the offices of the student-run newspaper, the *Michigan Daily*, where he soon became a reporter and an editor. While reporting for the *Daily*, Hayden's political consciousness was awakened. In following stories about a professor who was fired for his alleged Communist beliefs and about segregation in the fraternity system, Hayden realized that politics had a concrete impact on those around him.

Hayden's life away from the paper mirrored this awakening. While he had grown up as an obedient student who played by the rules, he was becoming a nonconformist at college. At that time, the role model for young rebels was beatnik writer Jack Kerouac, who wrote books about dropping out of mainstream society. Recalling this inspiration, Hayden says he and his friends "immersed ourselves in philosophy, kept our distance from the fraternity culture, rode motorcycles, and individually hitchhiked to all corners of America during vacation breaks."[21]

Hayden was not only the college student who was becoming politically active. Many students in the North supported the actions of the civil rights activists in the South. In Ann Arbor, a new student group called Students for a Democratic Society, or SDS, began organizing protests at local stores that refused to hire African Americans or that paid them substandard wages.

SDS was founded by a student named Robert Alan Haber, whose father was a professor at the University of Michigan. Haber's apartment was directly behind the offices of the *Daily*, and he soon struck up a friendship with Hayden. Although Hayden did not immediately join SDS, he found the political discussions he had with Haber to be very enlightening.

Inspired by Student Activists

Although Hayden was gradually becoming more politically aware, his development into a true radical accelerated in June 1960, when he traveled to California to cover the Democratic National Convention for the *Michigan Daily*. The convention, to be held in Los Angeles, would not open until August, so Hayden had plenty of time for a side trip to San Francisco. There he stepped into a maelstrom of political protest. Days before his arrival, the House Un-American Activities Committee (HUAC) traveled to San Francisco and held hearings at city hall to investigate the alleged Communist beliefs of public schoolteachers. Hundreds of students from the nearby University of California at Berkeley had traveled to San Francisco to protest the hearings. They were met by police dressed in riot gear. When students tried to disrupt the hearings by entering city hall, police turned fire hoses on the crowd. The powerful jets of water sent the protesters flying onto the street and pushed some through plate-glass windows of nearby buildings.

Following this incident, the students returned to Berkeley to plan more actions. At this point, having just arrived in town, Hayden met up with these activists as they were passing out political leaflets on campus. That day, he moved into the house where they coordinated their activities. During the next few weeks, Hayden was exposed to many new ideas as he spoke with these experienced political activists.

Upon the conclusion of the Democratic Convention, Hayden headed for home. On the way, he stopped in Minneapolis to attend a meeting of a group of activists known as the National Student Association. In attendance were black activists from the Student Nonviolent Coordinating Committee (SNCC). When Hayden met these young men and women, who had protested for civil rights in Southern states, he was moved by their tales of beatings and arrests. He recalled of these encounters:

The radical nature of Tom Hayden's activism resulted in criminal indictment and a five-year prison sentence.

They lived on a fuller level of feeling than any people I'd ever seen, partly because they were making modern history in a very personal way, and partly because by risking death they came to know the value of living each moment to the fullest. Looking back, this was a key turning point, the moment my political identity began to take shape. The student culture, exemplified by conformist fraternities and impersonal lecture halls back in Ann Arbor, had left me searching for more. . . . Here were the models of charismatic commitment I was seeking—I wanted to live like them.[22]

The Port Huron Statement

Politically energized, Hayden joined SDS upon his return to Ann Arbor. In 1961 he became the first field secretary for SDS, assisting in and reporting on the work of SNCC in the Deep South. The job took Hayden to McComb, Mississippi, a staunchly segregated town. There, he himself received a beating at the hands of white supremacists.

Upon his return to Ann Arbor, Hayden was convinced that white students across the country needed a central organization similar to SNCC in order to coordinate their political activities. He felt that if they joined together in this way it would give much more power to the voices of protest.

In June 1962 Hayden was poised to put his ideas in motion and turn SDS into a national organization. To facilitate this process, he and sixty other members of the organization met in Port Huron, Michigan, located fifty miles north of Detroit. One product of that meeting was a political manifesto, later known as the Port Huron Statement, which was meant to attract idealistic college students to SDS. It read, in part:

> We are people of this generation, bred in at least modest comfort, housed now in universities, looking uncomfortably to the world we inherit. . . . Our comfort was penetrated by events too troubling to dismiss. First, the permeating and victimizing fact of human degradation, symbolized by the Southern struggle against racial bigotry, compelled most of us from silence to activism. Second, the enclosing fact of the Cold War, symbolized by the presence of the [hydrogen] Bomb, brought awareness that we ourselves, and our friends, and millions of abstract "others" we knew more directly because of our common peril, might die at any time. . . .
>
> [We] began to see complicated and disturbing paradoxes in our surrounding America. The declaration of "all men are created equal . . ." rang hollow before the facts of Negro life in the South and the big cities of the North. The proclaimed peaceful intentions of the United States contradicted its economic and military investments in the Cold War status quo.[23]

The organizers of the meeting took the Port Huron Statement and began forming SDS chapters at college campuses across the country.

Vietnam Intrudes

The message of Hayden and SDS took on a new urgency when the United States greatly escalated military involvement in Vietnam in early 1965. On April 17, SDS held the first mass antiwar march of the 1960s in Washington, D.C. The group had expected a few thousand people to participate. More than twenty-five thousand showed up. In November another demonstration cosponsored by SDS drew thirty thousand.

Media reports on such events made SDS—and Tom Hayden—famous. SDS grew quickly and by the end of 1965 there were more than eighty chapters, with new ones forming every day on college campuses and even in some high schools. By 1968, SDS had over one hundred thousand members on four hundred campuses nationwide.

Hayden's prominence brought him to the attention of government officials in North Vietnam, who in December 1965 asked him and several other activists to visit their country. Hayden knew their purpose was to sway public opinion in the United States against the war, and this made him pause before agreeing to go. More than twenty-five years later, Hayden recalled his thoughts:

> Wasn't I supporting the enemy against our [soldiers]? Being for peace was one thing, but traveling to [North Vietnam capitol] Hanoi was quite another. Was I an American or a traitor? In my innocence . . . I thought that . . . the proposed trip was a very American thing to do and that the best way to support American soldiers was to end the killing.[24]

In Vietnam, Hayden met with government officials, toured factories, visited the countryside, and spent time with average citizens. He even met with an American prisoner of war (POW) whose plane had been shot down.

Upon his return to the United States Hayden was a celebrity. He was interviewed at length on several television shows and was featured in articles in the *New York Times* and in *Life* and *Time* magazines.

Radical Actions

As one of SDS's leaders, Hayden also found himself at the center of many protests, some of which turned violent. One such demonstration took place at Columbia University, in New York

City. Because scientists at colleges such as Columbia were engaged in weapons research, SDS had called for "the disruption, dislocation, and destruction of the military's access to manpower, intelligence, or resources [at] universities."[25] On April 23, SDS sponsored a rally to protest the school's membership in the Institute of Defense Analysis (IDA), an association of a dozen universities that advised the Department of Defense in matters of science, engineering, and other fields.

The rally turned into a full-fledged campus rebellion, with protesters taking over major buildings and temporarily holding several faculty members hostage. Hayden decided to travel to Columbia because he wanted to "participate in this new stage of student struggle."[26] For the next five days, Hayden was at the center of the protest, holding meetings and preparing students for the inevitable assault by police forces. The demonstration finally ended when police attacked the protesters with kicks, clubs, and tear gas.

In an article for *Ramparts* magazine, Hayden recalled that the takeover was meant as more than an antiwar demonstration:

> The students had fun, they sang and danced and wise-cracked, but there was continual tension. There was no question of their constant awareness of the seriousness of their acts. . . . There was a political message as well. . . . The Columbia students . . . want a new and independent university standing against the mainstream of American society, or they want no university at all.[27]

Bloody Confrontations

The student takeover at Columbia quickly set a new standard for protest, and similar actions followed on several other campuses. In fact, the student revolt was becoming so popular that by the middle of 1968 an opinion poll found that 19 percent of all American college students—about 1 million people—agreed with the statement that the United States needed a political party dedicated to revolution.

Such was the situation when the Democrats gathered in Chicago to choose a presidential candidate in August 1968. SDS and other antiwar groups planned massive protests. In response, the city leaders placed eleven thousand police on full alert. Six thousand National Guardsmen were brought in, and about seventy-five hundred U.S. Army troops and one thousand federal agents from the FBI, the CIA, and army and navy intelligence services were also on duty.

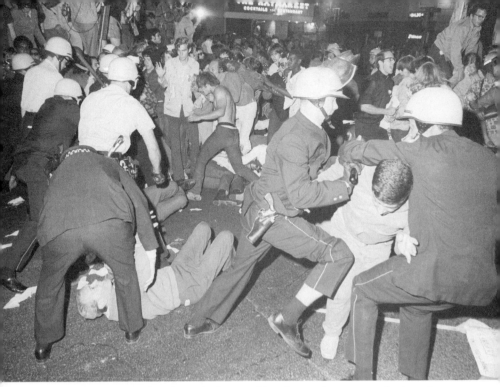

Demonstrators and police clash in a bloody confrontation during the 1968 Democratic National Convention in Chicago.

Hayden himself was constantly followed by two Chicago police officers who openly dogged his every step, following him to restaurants, to meetings, and even into public bathrooms.

Hayden wanted to prevent violence. To do so he spent his days with city officials trying to get permits to hold demonstrations. Try as he might, Hayden's efforts were rebuffed. SDS was denied parade permits, the use of a local stadium for a rally was nixed, and permits to demonstrate or camp in the city's parks were impossible to obtain. One protest leader wrote that the city officials "seemed determined to have a confrontation that can only produce violence and bloodshed."[28]

In the face of this intransigence, Hayden began planning for the inevitable confrontation. About one hundred student marshals were trained to use bullhorns in order to guide marchers and keep them in orderly lines. Others were trained in resistance tactics, learning to protect their faces and vital organs from clubs and kicks.

These techniques were put to the test moments before midnight on August 25, when police officers swept into Lincoln Park, where many protesters were gathered. Officers fired tear gas and began clubbing everyone in sight. Hayden describes the experience of being gassed: "It was as if someone held me down and stuffed pepper in my mouth, nose, and eyes. The impact made everyone . . . [run] blindly in whatever direction promised relief from the clouds of gas."[29]

Violence and arrests continued over the next few days. On August 28, the last night of the convention, a confrontation between protesters and the police occurred that shocked the entire nation. Hayden describes what he saw from his vantage point in the midst of the melee:

> We saw smoke and heard popping noises a split second before tear gas hit our front lines and began wafting upward into the Hilton and nearby hotels. We stopped, choking, trying to bite into our shirts. Then the [police] charged, chopping short strokes into the heads of people, trying to push us back. They knocked down and isolated several people, leaping on them for terrible revenge. . . . I got through the front lines and around the police to the very wall of the Hilton, where a mixed group of fifty or so . . . reporters, protestors, and—for all I knew—plain ordinary citizens, were standing frozen against the wall, between the hotel and the police, who were facing the oncoming marchers. When the marchers fell back, the police turned on our trapped crowd, moving in with a vengeance, clubs and Mace [tear gas] pointed at our faces. We instinctively joined arms. They started pulling off one person at a time, spraying Mace in their eyes, striking their kidneys or ribs with clubs, and tripping them. Their eyes were bulging with hate, and they were screaming with a sound that I had never heard from a human being. . . . Then, as people started staggering backward, someone kicked in the window behind us, and we fell through the shattered street-level opening to the Hilton's . . . Lounge. . . . The police leaped through the windows, going right by me, turning over tables in the swank lounge, scattering the drinkers, breaking glasses and tables.[30]

This violence was broadcast on live television watched by 90 million Americans. In a subsequent report, a presidential commission characterized the incident as a police riot.

Charged with Conspiracy

In the presidential election that November, Republican Richard M. Nixon was the winner. During the campaign, Nixon had promised to restore "law and order" to America's streets. In March 1969, months after his inauguration, Nixon's Justice Department charged Hayden and six others with conspiracy to incite violence in Chicago. FBI director J. Edgar Hoover, who had long sought to curtail antiwar protests, expressed his satisfaction saying. "A successful prosecution of this type would be a unique achievement."[31]

The trial of the "Chicago Seven," as they were called, commenced on September 24. The government attempted to prove that the Chicago riots were a carefully planned conspiracy by Hayden and the others. The defense countered that it was a spontaneous demonstration by large numbers of people who wanted to end the war.

The judge, seventy-four-year-old Julius Hoffman, consistently sided with the prosecutors. After a five-month trial, six of the defendants, including Hayden, were found guilty. Hayden was given a five-year prison sentence. He was released pending appeal, however, and on November 1, 1972, the U.S. Court of Appeals reversed the convictions, citing numerous errors committed by Judge Hoffman.

Life Changes

The reversal of the conviction allowed Hayden to get on with his life, which by this time included actress Jane Fonda. The actress

The "Chicago Seven" (Hayden is fifth from left) pose with their attorneys. The group was charged with conspiracy to incite violence at the 1968 Democratic National Convention in Chicago.

was rich and famous but was also a political activist who supported a number of causes such as civil rights, feminism, and opposition to the Vietnam War. The couple had met in 1971 at an antiwar rally in Ann Arbor, and they soon fell in love. Hayden describes how two people from such different backgrounds came together:

> The passion of our common involvement [in politics] no doubt caused our involvement in passion for each other. Being able to fight the same hazardous battles daily, and to do so *together* rather than in loneliness, was a powerful basis for this love.[32]

In January 1973 the couple married. By this time, popular public opinion had turned against the U.S. involvement in Vietnam, and by 1975 it was over. Hayden's ten-year quest for peace in Vietnam had succeeded.

After the war, Hayden came to believe that he could change the political system by working within it. In 1982 he ran successfully for the California state legislature. He served for ten years in the assembly; he was then elected to the state senate in 1992, where he served eight years. During this time he was the author of over 175 measures. Many of these were shaped by Hayden's liberal political beliefs and included reform of campaign financing, improvements in worker safety, prevention of domestic violence, lessening gang violence in the inner city, and protecting endangered species.

In 2000, term limits prevented Hayden from running again for state senator. In the following years, Hayden continued to write. In 2002, he published *Irish on the Inside: In Search of the Soul of Irish America*, a book about his quest to learn about his Irish ancestry. Hayden has also remained true to his basic values, choosing peace over violence, people over corporate profits, and education over ignorance. As national correspondent Nicholas Lemann wrote, "Tom Hayden changed America."[33]

CHAPTER 4

Cesar Chavez

Cesar Chavez is recognized today as having transformed the lives of millions of migrant farmworkers through nonviolent protest. Millions honor him for having led the struggle of farmworkers to earn a decent wage. However, Chavez spent many years simply trying to stay alive under a harsh system that paid him little and cared about him even less.

Cesar Estrada Chavez was born on March 31, 1927, near Yuma, Arizona. Cesar grew up surrounded by a large extended family of grandparents, uncles, aunts, and cousins who lived nearby. Cesar's parents, Librado and Juana, operated a small business consisting of a grocery store, an auto repair shop, a pool hall, and a candy counter. A substantial portion of the Chavezes' business came from their many relatives.

Lessons Learned

Life was good for the first several years of Cesar's life. Hardship came, however, when the Great Depression began in late 1929. Millions of Americans lost their jobs as the economy went into a tailspin. The patrons of the Chavez store were no exception. Suddenly, they had no money to buy food. Librado and Juana could not watch their relatives starve and sold food to them on credit for several years. By 1932, however, lack of paying customers left Librado and Juana unable to pay their bills. Eventually they were forced to sell their family business at a huge loss.

Fortunately for Cesar and his family, Librado also owned a farm outside Yuma, where they could live and grow their own food. Although many others were hungry, the Chavez family always had more than enough vegetables, eggs, milk, and chicken for their own use. When hungry beggars came to the farm, Juana often provided them with filling meals of beans, rice, and tortillas. The generosity his mother showed to the downtrodden made a lasting impression on Cesar.

Cesar's mother taught him other valuable lessons as well. From the time he was a small child, she showed him the importance of nonviolence. Instead of using fists when challenged, Juana told her

41

son, "God gave you senses, like your eyes and mind and tongue, so that you can get out of anything."[34] This was a hard lesson for young Cesar, especially when he started school, as he faced prejudice and discrimination that often pushed him to the brink of violence. For example, the white children frequently hurled racial insults at their Mexican American classmates. These taunts would often result in fistfights among the students. Although he most often resisted these fights, the confrontations caused him to develop a strong dislike of school. He preferred instead to spend his days happily helping with chores on the family farm.

"Like Being Nailed to a Cross"

Young Cesar's idyllic life on the family farm ended in 1933, when one of the worst droughts in history parched the lands in the western United States. The irrigation canals that the family depended on for water for their crops dried up. The crops they relied on for income dwindled and the family was unable to pay its annual property tax bill. By 1939 the bill had ballooned to such a large amount that the county seized the Chavez farm for nonpayment of property taxes.

Like thousands of other Americans similarly uprooted, the Chavez family loaded up whatever they could carry in their old car, leaving everything else behind. They headed for California to start anew.

California, however, was not the promised land the Chavezes had hoped for. The only work to be found was picking crops by hand in the hot sun, and even these jobs were scarce. When work was available, wages were so low, less than $2 a day per worker, that all four of Cesar's brothers and sisters had to help their parents pick crops from sunup to sundown just to earn enough money to survive. In *Cesar Chavez: Autobiography of La Causa*, Chavez described to Jacques E. Levy the arduous nature of the work they did:

> [Picking lettuce is] just like being nailed to a cross. You have to walk twisted, as you're stooping over, facing the row, and walking [at a right angle] to it. You are always trying to find the best position because you can't walk completely sideways, it's too difficult, and if you turn the other way, you can't [pick]. . . . Many [other] things in farm labor are terrible, like going under the [grape] vines that are sprayed with . . . pesticides. You have to touch those leaves and inhale that poison. Then there are heat

Throughout his career, civil rights activist Cesar Chavez organized a number of nonviolent protests to draw attention to the plight of millions of migrant farmworkers.

and short-handle hoes and stooping over. So many jobs require stooping. . . . All that stooping is why farm workers die before they're fifty.[35]

Backbreaking labor was only a part of the hardship. After work, laborers were forced to live in huge migrant worker camps where there was no running water, plumbing, or electricity. Hundreds of workers shared a single outdoor toilet, and diseases such as dysentery were rampant.

"Get Out if You Can"

If conditions in the migrant camps were hard, life became even harder between jobs, since the camps were only for those who were working. When the Chavezes had no work, the family lived in their dilapidated 1927 Studebaker, a car that Librado seemed miraculously able to repair and keep on the road. Chavez remembers the horrible living conditions endured by his family and others during that era: "[Workers] bathed and drank from irrigation

43

ditches. Many families often lived on riverbanks or under bridges, in shacks built of linoleum scraps and cardboard cartons, or tents improvised from [burlap] sacks."[36]

With his family constantly on the move, Cesar attended sixty-five separate elementary schools. Always there was racism to contend with. By eighth grade, fed up with prejudice and mistreatment at the hands of white teachers and students, he dropped out of school altogether.

The chance to escape, at least temporarily, from farm labor came in 1944, when Chavez joined the U.S. Navy. By this time, the Chavez family was living in Delano, in California's Central Valley. Chavez served for two years before returning to Delano. Upon his return, Chavez married his girlfriend, Helen Fabela. The couple then moved to San Jose and started a family. Although he was a veteran, Chavez's lack of a high school diploma prevented him from getting a good job. The only work he could find was picking string beans for $1 a day. With little money coming in, the Chavez family was able to afford to live only in a neighborhood, or barrio, so unpleasant that it was known as Sal Si Puedes, Spanish for "get out if you can."

Learning Nonviolence

About this time, a Roman Catholic priest named Donald McDonnell came to Sal Si Puedes to establish a new parish. The Chavez family was among the first to join McDonnell's congregation, and Cesar Chavez soon befriended the priest and helped him fix up a small building where he could hold Mass. McDonnell was more than a priest, however. He was also an activist who worked trying to improve living conditions of the local farmworkers. He and Chavez had long talks about civil rights and about how the great Indian leader Mohandas Gandhi had achieved independence for his nation using nonviolent protests.

In *César Chavez: A Triumph of Spirit*, Richard Griswold del Castillio and Richard A. Garcia describe the importance of Gandhi's teachings to Chavez:

> Gandhi spoke about the complete sacrifice of oneself for others, about the need for self-discipline . . . in order to achieve a higher good. These were values that Mexican farm workers could understand, not only in the life of Christ but in their own family experience. Especially important to Chavez's moral development were Gandhi's ideas on nonviolence: they echoed his mother's admonitions and teachings.[37]

44

Learning of Gandhi's experience inspired Chavez to believe that nonviolent protest might work to improve the lives of farmworkers. The chance to turn inspiration to action came in 1952, when Chavez attended a community meeting held by a political organizer named Fred Ross, who had worked for various civil rights organizations since the late 1930s. Ross had come to San Jose to set up the Community Service Organization (CSO) in order to register farmworkers to vote and elect sympathetic politicians. Ross offered Chavez a job as head of the CSO voter registration project in San Jose for $30 a week, far more than he could earn picking vegetables.

When they voted, Mexican Americans, or Chicanos, as they later came to be known, tended to vote Democratic, and for this reason local officials, who were usually Republican, resisted Chavez's efforts. According to Chavez, deputy registrars, those officials who file the paperwork for new voters,

As a child, Chavez worked alongside his family picking crops in California's Central Valley. There he witnessed firsthand the hardships the farmworkers endured.

were Republicans. They were organized to prevent Chicanos from voting. There were restrictions on everything. We couldn't speak Spanish while registering; we couldn't go door to door [to register voters]; we couldn't register except in daylight hours [when most people were working]; we couldn't register on Sundays.[38]

The National Farm Workers Association

Eventually Chavez had to conclude that although voter registration drives might enable people to vote for local officials, the real political influence was still held by large agribusiness companies that employed the majority of Chicanos in the farm districts. As Chavez states: "The power of the growers was backed by the power of the police, the courts, the state and federal laws, and the financial power of the big corporations."[39]

In September 1962 then, Chavez decided that the only way to offset this power was to start a union. The goal was to sign up workers and grow strong enough to plan a general farm strike within the next five years. Uprooting his family, which by this time consisted of Helen and their eight children, Chavez moved back to Delano to begin this difficult task.

Along with the aid of his children, Chavez walked door-to-door in the barrios handing out leaflets urging workers to join what he called the National Farm Workers Association (NFWA). Chavez spent the next three years signing up Chicano farmworkers and planning NFWA's next move. The moment came in September 1965, when growers in Southern California cut wages during the harvest. Filipino farmworkers, who worked side by side with Chicanos in the fields, decided to fight back. The Filipinos had their own union, the Agricultural Workers Organizing Committee (AWOC), which organized a strike and won. When the harvest moved north, about fifteen hundred members of AWOC went on strike against the grape growers in Delano. They were soon joined by the twelve hundred members of the NFWA who also went on strike.

Chavez was front and center of the strike, giving speeches, talking to reporters, and organizing activities. For example, beginning at four o'clock in the morning, men, women, and children picketed the fields of the region's second-largest grape grower, Schenley Industries, a company that produced liquor and wine. The strikers sang songs, carried signs, and chanted slogans until dark. Police, meanwhile, beat, teargassed, and arrested demonstrators.

The strike quickly became a celebrated cause. Chavez and his fellow strikers attracted the sympathies of white college students, civil rights activists, and even celebrities who for years had been working to better the living conditions for black Americans and who helped raise money for the strikers at rallies.

Schenley reacted to the strike by busing in nonunion workers from as far away as San Francisco. When these workers crossed picket lines, some strikers advocated beating them or shooting at the buses. Chavez argued that those who used violence would only be losers in the end, saying in one speech: "We are engaged in . . . [a] struggle for the freedom and dignity which poverty denies us. But it must not be a violent struggle, even if violence is used against us. Violence can only hurt our cause."[40]

The strike continued through a long, chilly winter, eventually attracting national attention. On March 14, 1966, a Senate subcommittee visited Delano to investigate living and working conditions

Chavez (center) marches in New York with the National Farm Workers Association (NFWA) to encourage consumers to boycott lettuce. Chavez founded the NFWA to represent farmworkers' interests.

of the farmworkers. One of the senators who visited was Robert Kennedy. The next day the senator held a hearing and took local police officials to task for arresting strikers without cause, thereby violating their constitutional rights. Later that day, Kennedy became the first senator to ever march on a picket line when he joined Chavez and other strikers at the DiGiorgio Fruit Corporation's forty-four-hundred-acre ranch.

Hoping to keep their cause in the public eye, the strikers decided to march three hundred miles from Delano to Sacramento, the California state capital. Although the march was ostensibly to protest farm labor working conditions, it quickly became a focus for all Spanish-speaking Californians to take their grievances to the state government. The longest protest march in U.S. history began on March 17, with Chavez leading sixty-six fellow strikers. By the time it reached Sacramento on Easter Sunday, the crowd had grown to ten thousand, with the original marchers limping along on blistered, bloody feet.

Although they were in pain, there was reason for celebration. Hearing that a bartender's union was going to support the strikers by refusing to sell Schenley wine, the company signed a contract with the NFWA. This document recognized the authority of the union, guaranteed an immediate raise of thirty-five cents an hour, and contained other benefits to the workers.

Grapes and Hunger

After this victory, the Mexican and Filipino farm unions merged to form the United Farm Workers Organizing Committee (UFWOC), led by Chavez. Many other growers continued to refuse to negotiate, however, so the strikes continued. The union's next target was Giumarra Farms, the largest grape grower in Delano. Other growers helped the company by selling Giumarra grapes in unmarked boxes. This caused the union to organize a boycott against all table grapes.

Chavez decided to take the boycott nationwide. Strikers, many of whom had never before left California's Central Valley, spread out to major cities in the United States and Canada. Wherever they went they would stand outside large grocery stores, where they urged customers not to buy grapes. Once again the strikers were joined by college students, civil rights activists, and members of other unions.

Although the grape boycott was inspiring to many of the young people who participated, it did little to change the practices of the growers. By the second year of the strike, some union members,

Chavez speaks out against the use of toxic chemicals on grapes in 1986. Earlier in his career, Chavez successfully pressured grape growers to raise workers' wages.

feeling that they were being ignored, advocated violence. Now Chavez felt he had to do something dramatic to return control of the situation. He decided to use one of Gandhi's tactics: a hunger strike. Chavez later recalled:

> I had to bring the Movement to a halt, do something that would force them and me to deal with the whole question of violence and ourselves. We had to stop long enough to take account of what we were doing. . . . So [on February 15, 1968] I stopped eating. . . . [I] was going to stop eating until such time as everyone in the strike either ignored me or made up their minds that they were not going to be committing violence.[41]

The hunger strike resulted in even more Chicanos joining the union. As word of Chavez's action spread, thousands of farmworkers gathered at the union headquarters in Delano to commit themselves to the cause of nonviolence.

The hunger strike drew worldwide attention to the grape boycott by the time Chavez finally ended the fast, on the twenty-fifth day. By 1969 the boycott went international, and fewer and fewer people were buying California table grapes. Finally one grape grower signed with the UFWOC. Several others followed, and by June 1970, most Delano grape growers had signed with the union. The workers returned to the fields, and within weeks, grapes carrying the union label began to flood into grocery stores across North America.

For the union's members, the contracts brought higher wages, safer working conditions, and little things that meant so much, such as fresh water and clean bathrooms in the fields. Chavez had paid a high price for the victory, however. His health was so bad from the hunger strike that he was forced to spend a year recuperating.

A Simple Pine Box

In the years that followed, Chavez saw his creation, now called the United Farm Workers (UFW), continue its work. In the early 1970s, the UFW organized strikes and boycotts to get higher wages from grape and lettuce growers. During the 1980s, Chavez led another boycott to protest the use of pesticides that often sickened farmworkers. He again fasted to draw public attention. These strikes and boycotts generally ended with the signing of agreements favorable to farmworkers.

Chavez continued to work while most men his age had retired. In frail health, on April 2, 1993, he traveled to San Luis, Arizona, only miles from the Yuma home where he was born, to testify in a court case. In the early morning hours of April 23, the sixty-six-year-old Chavez died in his sleep from natural causes. In the months before his death, he had told his family that he wanted a simple funeral. Respecting his wishes, Cesar Chavez was buried in a plain pine box. Thirty-five thousand people attended his funeral, including civil rights activist Jesse Jackson and members of the Kennedy family. Most of those attending, however, were simply workers, citizens, and supporters who had fought side by side with the man who, more than anyone else, brought justice and dignity to the farmworkers of California and beyond.

CHAPTER 5

Betty Friedan

Betty Friedan is known as the mother of the modern feminist movement. She was born in an era when there were few options for American women, other than marriage and family. Yet because of her political activism, women have gained a wide range of career choices that simply did not exist before.

Betty Friedan was born Betty Naomi Goldstein in Peoria, Illinois, on February 4, 1921. Her father, Harry, owned the most prestigious jewelry store in Peoria. His success allowed Betty, the oldest of three, to grow up in very comfortable circumstances, with servants to take care of the housework.

Betty was Harry's pride and joy. She liked to write, and he encouraged her. He so valued her childhood poetry that he saved her poems in the huge safe at his store. While Harry showered affection on her, Betty's mother, Miriam, did not. A beautiful,

Feminist activist Betty Friedan grew up in an era when the only options available to American women were marriage and family.

pampered woman who spent hours on her appearance, Miriam was highly critical of Betty. As she recalls in her autobiography, *Life So Far*, Betty therefore thought of herself as a "mess, clumsy, inadequate, bad, naughty, ugly. . . . "[42]

Miriam criticized her daughter despite the fact that Betty was a genius who was certified in high school to have an IQ of 180 points. She excelled academically, and her love of writing led her to become a reporter for her school newspaper. Still, Betty had a difficult time socially. She was not pretty and was never asked out on dates. As her brother, Harry Jr., says: "When Betty was in high school she was ugly and had no boyfriends. She was popular and well-liked—fellows *liked* her . . . [but] she felt ostracized."[43]

Betty had reason to feel ostracized. The Goldsteins were Jewish, whereas most of Peoria's residents were Gentiles. The children were not invited to join the high school sororities and fraternities popular at that time. Betty later spoke of this rejection in an interview with *New York Times* reporter Paul Wilkes in 1970: "I guess Peoria is where my awareness of injustices in minority groups and a passionate concern for them was born. My father often told me the people friendly to him in business wouldn't speak to him after sundown [because he was Jewish]."[44]

Political Awakening

In a time when most American women did not work outside the home, Betty knew that she wanted more than the life of a homemaker. She wanted an absorbing career. To pursue this dream, she enrolled at Smith College in 1938. Smith was an all-women's college in western Massachusetts and a haven for high achievers like Betty Goldstein. Friedan later recalled that finding acceptance from other women with similar dreams changed her. She became more accepting of herself, far from the criticism of her mother and Peoria's small-town attitudes.

Goldstein graduated from Smith in 1942 with high honors and a degree in psychology. She then continued her studies, attending graduate school at the University of California at Berkeley, where she won an academic fellowship to complete her PhD. The prize came with a price, however. By this time, Goldstein had a boyfriend, but he was intimidated by her intelligence. He told her: "It's over between us. I'm never going to win a fellowship like that."[45] Around the same time, Goldstein's father died. These two losses hit her hard. With a broken heart, she decided to leave the academic world and turn down the fellowship.

Goldstein hoped to find a job that would allow her to combine her love of writing with her deeply felt sense of social justice. At that time, there was strong political activism within the labor unions in New York City. Goldstein moved there and began writing for *U.E. News*, the newspaper of the United Electrical Workers (UE) union. While working there, she had her first direct exposure to issues concerning women, when she wrote a piece about how the UE fought to end job discrimination against women. During this period, Betty met Carl Friedan, an intelligent, charming actor. In 1947 the couple was married, and the next year their first child was born.

Betty Friedan eventually found herself the victim of sex discrimination. The *U.E. News* had no policy of granting maternity leave, and when she became pregnant with her second child, she was fired. This was her first overt experience with sex discrimination. As she writes: "There was no word for sex discrimination then, no law against it. But I bitterly felt the injustice of it, being fired because I was pregnant."[46]

By this time, her husband had abandoned the uncertain world of theater and was working in advertising. When Friedan was pregnant with their third child in 1956, the family moved to the suburbs. Now Friedan had become a seemingly typical stay-at-home mother, raising a family in a suburb of New York City.

"The Problem That Has No Name"

Although she was busy with her family, Friedan continued to write, producing freelance articles for women's magazines. At about this same time, Friedan observed an interesting phenomenon. While attending the fifteenth reunion of her Smith College class in 1957, Friedan noticed that her old friends talked mostly about their husbands and children, rather than about personal feelings. Friedan was fascinated and wanted to discover how these women felt about themselves. With the help of several friends, she put together a questionnaire entitled "What Kind of Woman Are You?" The survey was filled with provocative questions such as "To what extent do you talk to your husband about your deepest feelings? . . . Is your sex life less important than it used to be? . . . Were you depressed after [giving] birth? . . . As a mother do you feel . . . [m]artyred? . . . What part of housekeeping do you . . . [d]etest? . . . Have you ever taken a public stand about a controversial issue?"[47]

From the survey, Friedan discovered that, in spite of their general prosperity and seemingly well-adjusted lives, many women

Friedan spent five years writing her best seller The Feminine Mystique. *The book explores the many prejudices American women face.*

were bored, unhappy, and vaguely suffering from what Friedan soon labeled "the problem that has no name."[48]

The questionnaire led Friedan to write an article titled "Are Women Wasting Their Time in College?" in which she pointed out that despite their education, many women felt unfulfilled while performing the daily tasks of a stay-at-home mother. Women's magazines refused to publish the article, however. The editor at *Redbook* wrote Friedan's agent and said the author "must be going off her rocker. Only the most neurotic housewife will identify with this."[49] Fortunately for Friedan, she was able to sell the concept to an editor of a large publishing company. She was given a $3,000 advance, and for the next five years she worked on a book about what she called the "feminine mystique."

Friedan completed *The Feminine Mystique* in 1963. She explained the meaning behind the title of her book in an article in a 1970 issue of *TV Guide*:

> The feminine mystique is the name I have given to a way of looking at woman that has become epidemic in America during the last 15 years. Based on old prejudices disguised in new . . . dogmas, it defines woman solely in sexual terms, as man's wife, mother, love object, dishwasher and general server of physical needs, and never in

human terms, as a person herself. It glorifies woman's only purpose as the fulfillment of her "femininity" through sexual passivity, loving service of husband and children, and dependence on man for all decisions in the world outside the home: "man's world." [50]

The Feminine Mystique struck a chord with millions of women, becoming an instant best seller, and Friedan was suddenly seen as speaking for all American women. She appeared on television shows and was featured in national magazine articles. Friedan's success allowed her and her family to leave suburbia and move to New York City. The best-selling author set out on a whirlwind of book signings, lectures, and television appearances.

Founding a National Organization for Women

The Feminine Mystique was published at a time when the federal government's role in American society was rapidly expanding. In 1964, Congress passed the Civil Rights Act aimed at eliminating discrimination against African Americans. The bill's authors, however, went further: Title VII of the Act specifically barred employment discrimination on the basis of gender as well as race. To enforce Title VII, the bill established the Equal Employment Opportunity Commission (EEOC) to hear complaints from people who believed they had experienced bias in the workplace.

The newly created EEOC had to deal with a host of issues never before examined by a federal agency. For example, at that time, help wanted ads had separate "Help Wanted—Male" and "Help Wanted—Female" columns. Some felt this discriminated against women by keeping them out of jobs, many of which were higher paying, traditionally performed by men. In addition, state laws prevented women from working in certain occupations, limited the number of hours they could work, and limited the amount of weight they could lift. Employers were also allowed to control women's private lives. Schoolteachers, for example, could be fired if they became pregnant. Flight attendants could be kept off of airplanes if they gained too much weight, reached the age of thirty-two, or even got married.

Despite the federal government's supposed commitment to fairness to women, when Friedan began to study the actions of the EEOC, she realized that the agency was concerned more with racial, rather than gender, bias. As the EEOC lawyer Sunny Pressman told Friedan: "It's like some secret order has been given not to do battle on the sex discrimination part of Title VII. We're getting hundreds, thousands of complaints, but nobody [at the EEOC] is supposed to do anything about them. You've got to expose it." [51]

In 1966, in order to prod the EEOC into action, Friedan and twenty-eight other women each contributed $5 as a seed fund to start what they called the National Organization for Women (NOW). The first NOW meeting was held at Friedan's New York apartment, and she was elected president of the organization. To clearly state the organization's goals, Friedan composed the first sentence of NOW's Statement of Purposes, words considered quite radical at the time: "[NOW has been founded] to take action, to bring women into full participation in the mainstream of American society now, exercising all the privileges and responsibilities thereof in truly equal partnership with men." [52]

Friedan discusses the mission of the National Organization for Women (NOW) with reporters. She founded NOW in 1966 to help promote equal rights for women.

Death Threats and Division

Even during its earliest years, NOW created controversy. In 1967, as a spokeswoman for the organization, Friedan advocated sex education in public schools and called for the repeal of all laws restricting abortions. These positions attracted the organized opposition of right-wing groups such as the John Birch Society, the Christian Crusade, and others who unleashed a torrent of pent-up hatred against Friedan and the movement she had created.

Friedan started to receive piles of hate mail and several death threats a week. Typical of those was a letter delivered to her before she was scheduled to give a lecture and book signing at Dayton's department store in Minneapolis. It read, "You communist Jew, you set foot in Dayton's and we'll bomb the building."[53] (The lecture was canceled by authorities in response.)

There were also divisions within NOW, as some younger women began to press the organization to take positions that Friedan believed were hurting the feminist cause among middle-class women. For example, Friedan says that lesbians "started disrupting lectures I was giving in the late sixties and demanding equal time to further their agenda. . . . I did not take kindly to extremists who tried to take over the stage and insist on talking about lesbians. I didn't want to discuss lesbianism. . . . The audience had come to hear about issues . . . facing all women."[54]

Refusing to compromise on such issues, Friedan became unpopular, especially among the younger faction of the organization. Therefore, when her term as president was up, she did not seek reelection. Not one to leave the stage quietly, in March 1970, while giving her final speech as NOW president, Friedan called for a women's strike to be held on August 26, 1970, the fiftieth anniversary of the passage of the nineteenth Amendment, which guaranteed women the right to vote. She told the cheering crowd:

> I propose that the women who are doing menial chores in the offices cover their typewriters and close their notebooks, that the telephone operators unplug their switchboards, the waitresses stop waiting, cleaning women stop cleaning, and everyone who is doing a job for which a man would be paid more—stop—and every woman pegged forever as assistant, doing jobs for which men get the credit—stop. . . . And by the time those twenty-four hours are ended, our revolution will be a fact.[55]

Although NOW had only four months to organize the strike, it was a stunning success. More than fifty thousand women walked off their jobs to protest in New York City alone. Fifteen thousand demonstrated in Chicago, twenty-five thousand in Los Angeles; smaller crowds of women marched in other cities. By the time the day was over, thousands of women who had attended the protests had also joined NOW for the first time. As Judith Hennessee writes in *Betty Friedan: Her Life:* "August 26, 1970 may well have been the most glorious day in Betty's life. Never again would she lead such a united group in such a euphoric spirit, never again would she be regarded with such universal good will. Women said afterwards that the march had been the most thrilling thing in their lives."[56]

Controversy over Equal Rights

In four short years, NOW had put women's issues at the top of the national agenda. But Friedan was only beginning. In 1971 she founded a new organization, National Women's Political Caucus (NWPC) to lobby congressional leaders to pass the Equal Rights Amendment (ERA) to the Constitution. The amendment, which had first been proposed in 1923, read: "Equality of rights under the law shall not be denied or abridged by the United States or any state on account of sex."[57]

One year later, in 1972, both houses of Congress voted in favor of the ERA. But for the ERA to become part of the Constitution it also had to be ratified by three-quarters of the states—thirty-eight states in seven years. A firestorm of opposition at the state level arose. Corporate executives claimed bankruptcy would result if women were paid as much as men. Military leaders expressed fear that the ERA would force them to use women in combat roles. Some opponents even argued that the amendment would force women and men to use the same public restrooms. Such opposition ultimately would doom the ERA. Although Congress passed an extension of the time limit for ratification, the ERA died when only thirty-five states voted in favor of it.

In the intervening years, Friedan continued her activism on other fronts. Feeling that women had to have more control over when they had children, she was responsible for founding the National Abortion Rights Action League (NARAL). This group used the courts to fight state and federal laws that restricted abortion. Three years later, NARAL lawyers played a role in the Supreme Court's striking down all abortion laws in the United States.

Friedan continued to champion civil rights as an older woman. In the 1980s she began to focus her attention on the problem of age discrimination in the United States.

It Changed My Life

Throughout the rest of the seventies, Friedan continued her efforts to end gender discrimination. She also continued writing magazine articles and books. In her 1976 book *It Changed My Life,* Friedan related the stories of hundreds of women who had written to her—or simply stopped her on the street—to tell her how the women's movement had changed their lives.

As Friedan grew older, even though many women her age might have considered retiring, Friedan found a new cause. In the late 1980s, she founded a project called the Fountain of Age, to fight the discrimination faced by older people. Friedan wrote a well-received book, *The Fountain of Age*, in which she examined the ways that senior citizens thought about love, family, responsibility, money, and other issues.

Betty Friedan has broadened opportunities for women. Because of her efforts, millions of women have been inspired to obtain college educations and to pursue fulfilling careers. Today, women who enter medicine, law, public safety, business, politics, and aerospace, to name just a few fields, owe a debt to Betty Friedan, who used her energies to bring equality to all.

CHAPTER 6

Abbie Hoffman

Abbie Hoffman was one of the most colorful—and controversial—characters of the 1960s. Part clown and part revolutionary, Hoffman was a master at media manipulation. Hoffman and his fellow Yippies managed to make headlines with their outrageous stunts and provocative statements about war, peace, and injustice. While his antics failed to sway the opinions of a majority of Americans, he managed to frighten the authorities. He also gained the adoration of millions of young people as what author Jonah Raskin calls "the first American cultural revolutionary in the age of television."[58]

"Hell Unleashed"

Abbot Howard Hoffman was born on November 30, 1936, in Worcester, Massachusetts. His father, known as Johnnie, worked near the family apartment as a pharmacist in his brother's drugstore. His mother, Florence, was a housewife.

Abbie was a difficult child. He was extremely jealous of his younger brother, Jack, and always demanded to be the center of attention. This led Johnnie to call him "hell unleashed."[59] By the time he was in middle school, Abbie was a notorious neighborhood troublemaker. He shoplifted cigarettes, drank alcohol, called teachers by their first names, cracked jokes during class, and beat up smaller kids. Few teenagers acted this way at the time, as Raskin writes: "By today's standards his bad behavior seems tame, but in Worcester in the late forties and early fifties his rebellion from middle-class Jewish traditions and values was unusual."[60]

When he got older, Hoffman adopted the "greaser" persona made popular by Marlon Brando in the 1953 movie about the rebellious leader of a motorcycle gang, *The Wild One*. Hoffman bought a motorcycle, wore black leather jackets, and raced up and down the streets of Worcester. He cut school to hustle pool or to bet at the horse track. Eventually he took to stealing cars and starting vicious fights with rivals.

New Ideas

Although he was a troublesome teen, Hoffman was also very smart, achieving As in most of his classes. As a result he was accepted at the highly selective Brandeis University in Waltham, Massachusetts. Many of the teachers at Brandeis at that time were well known for their liberal and even radical philosophies. One of those professors was Herbert Marcuse, an internationally recognized Marxist philosopher. Hoffman was immediately taken with Marcuse. He later wrote of his reaction to one of Marcuse's lectures, "Every new idea hit [me] like a thunderclap."[61]

Another major influence on Hoffman at this time was Sheila Karklin, an artist who danced to jazz and dressed like a beatnik—that is, all in black. The two started dating and, under her guidance, Hoffman gave up his greaser look and took to wearing a beret, blue jeans, and boots.

Abbie Hoffman was one of the most flamboyant activists of the 1960s. He often staged unconventional stunts in public to draw media attention to his causes.

As had been the case in high school, Hoffman proved both his intelligence and his leadership abilities. By the time he graduated in 1959, Hoffman was president of the school psychology club and captain of the school's tennis team. That fall he enrolled in graduate school at the University of California at Berkeley.

Politics, Protests, and Punishment

It was at Berkeley that Hoffman was first exposed to the world of political protests and demonstrations. In May 1960 the House Un-American Activities Committee (HUAC) arrived in San Francisco to hold hearings about alleged subversive activities by local schoolteachers. Hoffman, along with busloads of other Berkeley students, traveled to San Francisco to attend the hearings at city hall. When they were denied admission, they crowded onto the steps of the building and began chanting, "Down with HUAC!" [62]

Police reacted with force, using high-pressure water hoses and billy clubs, as Hoffman relates:

> The force of the water hoses drove people smashing into plate-glass windows. Students were clubbed to the ground, thrown off balconies, and kicked in the face. A pregnant woman was thrown down a flight of stairs. All around there was panic. . . . I was separated from those I came with. People ran into stores. The tall black-leather shapes [of the police] pursued, swinging their sticks. Sirens wailed all around. Screams filled the air. I ran through the side streets toward the theater district. . . . Four blocks from the riot, everything was as it always was. . . . No one seemed aware that the century's most turbulent decade had just begun. [63]

This clash proved to be a turning point in Hoffman's life and radicalized him politically. As a former street scrapper, Hoffman was excited by the violence. He told a fellow student: "It was spectacular. I loved it! The water, the fire hoses, the goons. It was like a . . . movie, fabulous!" [64]

"A Long Running Start"

Hoffman did not stay long in Berkeley. Instead, he returned to Worcester to marry Sheila. Before many years had passed they had two children. Hoffman, to support his growing family, took a job as a pharmaceutical salesman.

Hoffman did not abandon his political activism, however, and spent most of his free time working for various civil rights groups in Worcester's black neighborhood. He and fellow demonstrators picketed local businesses that would not hire blacks, and sometimes he was arrested. During this time, Hoffman's dedication earned him the nickname "Mr. Civil Rights."

In late 1965 Hoffman reached another turning point in his life after he was given a large dose of LSD by a friend. He spent ten hours experiencing strong hallucinations. Hoffman continued to use LSD; before long, he and his friends were taking the hallucinogen as well as smoking marijuana as often as possible.

Hoffman's drug use weakened further a marriage that had been rocky from the beginning. In 1966 Abbe and Sheila divorced. Around the same time, Hoffman was fired from his job at the pharmaceutical company. Freed of his ties to conventional society, Hoffman was ready to join the counterculture. This was an era when people wore buttons that said, "Don't trust anyone over thirty." Hoffman, however, was older than most hippies, as brother Jack Hoffman writes with Daniel Simon in *Run Run Run: The Lives of Abbie Hoffman*:

> He was off to find the '60s, and now, finally, the new youth culture he was looking for was out there and ready for him. The irony was that Abbie, who will always be associated in our minds with that youth culture, was turning thirty now and a good ten years older than most of the people who would share it with him, and ten years politically more experienced. By the time the youth of America began to awaken to the anti-war movement and the counterculture that went with it, Abbie had had a long running start.[65]

Making the Outrageous Commonplace

Hoffman left his tidy Worcester home and moved to a dirty tenement on New York's Lower East Side. Rats, poverty, overflowing trash cans, and heroin addicts were part of the street scene at that time. In the spring of 1967, Hoffman fell in with full-time antiwar activists who worked out of a loft on Beckman Street. He patiently listened to their ideas for marches and sit-ins, but he had his own ideas for changing society, ones that involved a broad, revolutionary makeover. He later recalled that part of his strategy was to turn mass media to his own purposes:

> A modern revolutionary group headed for the television station. . . . Information was culture and change in society would come when the information changed. We would

Hoffman's outrageous behavior in his support of politically liberal causes often resulted in his arrest.

make what was irrelevant relevant. What was outrageous, commonplace. Like freaked-out [revolutionaries], we would build a new culture smack-dab in the burned-out shell of the old dinosaur.[66]

While pondering ways to change the world, Hoffman decided that people placed too much importance on money. Hoffman began to advocate doing away with money, saying "free" was the "most revolutionary thing in America today. Free dance, free food, free theater, . . . free stores, free bus rides, free dope, free housing, and most important free money."[67] He urged people to destroy money, burn it, give it away, and roll joints with it.

In keeping with this theme, in May 1967, Hoffman and eighteen other political activists concocted a stunt to show how money could make seemingly respectable people do ridiculous things. The group entered the New York Stock Exchange and began clowning around, kissing, hugging, and eating money. Then they started to throw handfuls of one and five dollar bills off the balcony above the trading floor. Stock trading was halted as dozens of exchange employees fell over one another to grab at the money. When police tried to forcibly remove the group, the traders booed.

Hoffman had not notified the press of his plans. Journalists present to report on the stock trading observed it, however, and that evening Hoffman's actions were featured on television news programs across the country. This reinforced Hoffman's belief that outrageous actions could generate instant headlines.

Raising the Pentagon

Around this time, Hoffman met Anita Kushner. It was love at first sight, and the two were married on June 15, 1967, at a hippie wedding ceremony in Central Park. Along with several others, the couple soon began planning a project that was guaranteed to make the news: During an October antiwar demonstration, Hoffman told the press, he would surround the Pentagon with protesters who would chant and "levitate" the building one hundred feet in the air to shake out all the evil.

Hoffman used his notoriety as a controversial media figure to book activists dressed as witches to talk about the event on New York–based TV talk shows. He also invited the press to a theatrical demonstration in which a model of the Pentagon was lifted from a stage—with wires—as smoke bombs went off and psychedelic music played. The most attention was given to a claim Hoffman made that a drug called LACE was going to be handed out at the demonstration. This was supposed to cause people—including the police—to rip their clothes off and have sex. The claim was a hoax, but media took this seriously and stories about LACE were put forth on dozens of news shows. Hoffman considered such stunts to be good advertisements for the march on the Pentagon.

On Saturday, October 21, one hundred thousand people arrived in Washington, D.C., to participate in a week of activities organized by national antiwar organizations. By nightfall, about fifty thousand protesters had circled the Pentagon, face-to-face with tens of thousands of heavily armed U.S. marshals, National Guard troops, and paratroopers. The standoff lasted all night as protesters were arrested and hauled off by police. The levitation that Hoffman had promised never occurred, although he later wrote a description of the demonstration in which he claimed that it had.

"The Yippies Are Coming"

Almost immediately after the October protest, Hoffman began planning a major demonstration to coincide with the 1968 Democratic Convention, scheduled to be held in Chicago in August.

By this time, Hoffman was practically inseparable from Jerry Rubin, a fellow revolutionary who also practiced street theater and outrageous stunts to garner media attention. On the last day of 1967, Rubin, satirist Paul Krassner, and Abbie and Anita Hoffman formed a new organization to demonstrate in Chicago—a group called the Youth International Party, or Yippies, to perpetrate outrageous political stunts. Rubin predicted that within a few months "yippie" would become a household word, and his marketing instincts were correct. By spreading the word in antiwar "underground" newspapers, yippie quickly became a national buzzword. Within one month, *Newsweek* headlines blared "The Yippies are Coming!"[68] to Chicago.

The Yippies planned an event during the convention called the Festival of Life. Hoffman later recalled his fantasy of activities the Yippies would engage in, though none of them came to pass:

> [The] Democrats would gather in Chicago for a convention of death; in juxtaposition, we would gather to celebrate life. . . . We would secure a large park, sponsor workshops, exhibits, demonstrations and rock concerts in contrast to the deadly doldrums that would go on inside [the] Convention Hall. . . . [Our] strategy did not include plans for organized violence or riot although our fanciful literature carried our dope-induced hallucinations. We revealed that the Potheads' Benevolent Association had been busy all spring strewing [marijuana] seeds in the vacant lots of Chicago, anticipating the ideal growing weather of the predicted Long Hot Summer [of urban riots]. We spread the rumor that battalions of super-potent yippie males were getting in shape to seduce female convention-goers and that yippie agents were posing as hookers. There was no end to our nefarious plans. We would dress up people like Viet Cong and send them into the streets to shake hands like ordinary American politicians. We would paint cars taxi-yellow, pick up delegates and drop them in Wisconsin.[69]

Although Hoffman and Rubin approached the protests with biting humor, authorities were not laughing. Rumors abounded in the press that the Yippies were planning to assassinate Chicago mayor Richard J. Daley, dump LSD in the municipal water supply, and take over the control tower at O'Hare International Airport. Although few believed that the activists were capable of such activities, according to the editors of *A Nation Divided,* Clark

Dougan and Samuel Lipsman, "Only two kinds of people could take [Hoffman and] Rubin seriously, the police and television reporters."[70]

During the late August convention, police and protesters clashed repeatedly and often violently. Hoffman gave speeches, rallied the protesters, and attended meetings to organize resistance to the police. On August 28, the final day of the convention, he was finally arrested. While most protesters were bailed out within a few hours, police moved Hoffman from precinct to precinct, and from cell to cell for thirteen hours. He was not allowed to see lawyers or use a telephone. By the time he was released, the battles were over.

Conspiracy Trial

In the wake of the massive Chicago protests, Hoffman, along with six other activists, was indicted for conspiracy to incite violence at the Democratic Convention. When the trial commenced in September 1969, Hoffman decided to approach the courtroom as if it

Jerry Rubin (left) and Hoffman, seen here in 1984, were inseparable during the late sixties. Together they founded the Yippies, a political group who were known for their nefarious activities.

were a stage—or a circus ring. On the first day of the trial, he was photographed doing a full front flip on the courthouse steps. When introduced to the jury as the trial started, he blew a kiss. He infuriated the judge, Julius Hoffman (no relation), by placing Vietcong and American flags on the table where he sat. His goal, he later wrote, was to "demonstrate that we neither feared the court's power nor were impressed with the pomp and circumstance of tradition. . . . The Chicago Conspiracy Trial became . . . the greatest comedy . . . ever to occur in a courtroom."[71]

Such actions enraged the judge who, after six of the seven defendants were found guilty, sentenced them to federal prison. For inexplicable reasons, Hoffman, who had been the most disruptive at the trial, received the shortest sentence, eight months. However, a federal appeals court ruled that Judge Hoffman had been biased in favor of the prosecution and overturned all the convictions. Although he walked free, Hoffman's troubles were just beginning.

Life on the Run

By 1970 Hoffman was an infamous revolutionary. He was invited to speak at hundreds of college campuses. These events were often canceled, however, by college administrators and local authorities who did not want Hoffman in their community. When he defied such bans, he was often arrested for trespassing and other offenses. Hoffman fought these arrests on free speech grounds, and spent large sums of money on lawyers, bail, and fines.

In 1973, as the Vietnam War wound down and the antiwar movement splintered, Hoffman seemed adrift. Money from his books and speaking engagements was gone. With his career as a professional revolutionary at an end, Hoffman needed money, so he decided to write a book about the lives of drug dealers.

Hoffman later claimed that he was researching this book when he was arrested in August 1973, for trying to sell almost three pounds of cocaine to undercover New York police officers. Bail was set at two hundred thousand dollars, and Hoffman faced a mandatory sentence of fifteen years to life if convicted. Hoffman jumped bail and disappeared, eluding arrest for nearly seven years. During this time he became an environmental activist. He changed his appearance with plastic surgery and adopted the name Barry Freed. In 1980, however, he turned himself in to authorities in exchange for a reduced sentence, spending a few months in prison.

After his release in 1982, Hoffman wrote several popular books including an autobiography and a book about environmental activism. Hoffman suffered from bipolar syndrome, what is popularly

Hoffman smiles at a peace rally in Washington, D.C., in 1987. Throughout the 1980s Hoffman suffered from manic depression, and in 1989 he committed suicide.

called manic depression, however. While the manic episodes of the mental illness had driven him to revolutionary fame in the sixties, by the late eighties it was clinical depression that ruled his life. On April 12, 1989, the fifty-two-year-old Hoffman was found dead in his home in New Hope, Pennsylvania. Authorities said he had taken 150 powerful barbiturates and washed them down with whiskey. He left no suicide note. Several days later, a memorial in Worcester thrown by his family attracted six thousand people. At the funeral, speaker after speaker remembered Hoffman as fearless, flamboyant, and funny—an activist and a social radical who epitomized the revolutionary politics of the 1960s.

CHAPTER 7

Angela Davis

In the late 1960s, few activists aroused the combination of fear and admiration as Angela Davis. Her stately bearing and obvious intelligence made even her enemies take notice. While many heard her virulent antiestablishment rhetoric and feared the Black Power that she advocated, others praised her commitment to the African American community. Both as a Black Panther and as a college professor, Davis became a lightning rod for controversy and a symbol of change.

Angela Yvonne Davis was born into violent times in Birmingham, Alabama, on January 26, 1944. When she was very young, hers became the first African American family to move into an all-white neighborhood. When other black families followed, racists called "night riders" would throw bombs onto the porches of the new arrivals. These bombings were so relentless that the neighborhood earned the nickname of "Dynamite Hill." Those bombings also terrified the four-year-old Angela, who later told *Ebony* magazine:

> The first real vivid memory that I have of my childhood is the sound of a bomb exploding across the street from our house, and our whole house shaking and things falling. . . . Growing up in the South, growing up in a place like Birmingham, gives you a kind of immediate experience of oppression and racism that you wouldn't necessarily have had in [another] place.[72]

While they lived under segregation in the Deep South, the Davis family did not live in poverty. Angela's mother, Sally, was a schoolteacher in Birmingham, while her father, B. Frank Davis, was a former schoolteacher who operated a prosperous service station, also in Birmingham.

The bombings perpetrated by the night riders caused Angela to develop an early loathing for white people. Sally, who had worked with whites to fight segregation while in college, tried to change her daughter's mind and teach her tolerance. Davis writes in her autobiography:

Angela Davis's passion for militant black activism made her one of the most controversial activists of the 1960s.

> Through [mother's] political work, she had learned that it was possible for white people to walk out of their skin and respond with the integrity of human beings. She tried hard to make her little girl—so full of hatred and confusion—see white people . . . in terms of their potential . . . [in] a future world of harmony and equality. I didn't know what she was talking about.[73]

An A Student

In addition to lessons in tolerance, Angela was taught to read by Sally at a very young age. By the time she was in school, Angela was a voracious reader and a serious student who earned straight As. In 1959, when she was fifteen, Angela was one of only three black students out of thirty-five picked by a charitable organization, the American Friends Service committee, to receive a scholarship. This opportunity, based on her outstanding scholastic achievement, allowed her to move to New York City and study at Elizabeth Irwin High, a private school in Greenwich Village.

While attending Elizabeth Irwin High, Angela was first exposed to controversial political ideas shunned in the South. The *Communist Manifesto*, written in 1848 by German philosophers Karl Marx and Friedrich Engels, made a particular impression on the young woman. Marx and Engels wrote that all conflicts in history have been, at their core, struggles between the classes. The proletariat, or working classes who made up the majority of people, have been repressed by a much smaller number of bosses, managers, and rulers so that the latter can profit. Angela saw this division in society manifested in the relations between black and white people. She later recalled: "[What] moved me most . . . was the vision of a new society, without exploiters and exploited, a society without classes, a society where no one would be permitted to own so much that he could use his possessions to exploit other human beings."[74]

In response, Angela declared herself to be a Communist. She joined a Marxist youth organization called Advance, although she kept her new political beliefs to herself at school. She was remembered by fellow student Amy Saltz as "a total nebbish—she never said anything; she never did anything. . . . [She was] a very, very, shy, quiet girl . . . totally nondescript . . . [not] political at all."[75]

The shy, black student from Alabama, however, was determined, strong, and smart. By the time she graduated high school in 1961, she had been accepted by three of the six colleges she applied to. She chose Brandeis, in Waltham, Massachusetts, because it offered her a four-year scholarship at $1,500 per year, which was enough to cover most, if not all, her expenses for a college degree.

"Everywhere There Were Upheavals"

Davis majored in French literature at Brandeis and became fluent in the language. During her junior year, she took the opportunity to study for a year at the highly respected Sorbonne University of Paris. She spent her evenings in sidewalk cafes discussing revolutionary politics with like-minded students. Upon her return to the United States, Davis delivered an award-winning thesis on the French Revolution. In 1965, when she graduated with the highest academic honors, her French professor Murray Sachs described her as "one of the two or three best students I ever had."[76]

After graduating from Brandeis, Davis traveled to Germany to study philosophy at the Institute of Social Research at Johann Wolfgang von Goethe University in Frankfurt, West Germany. She became fluent in German in a remarkably short period and was able to master the complex theories of philosophers such as Immanuel Kant and Georg Hegel with equally impressive speed. Her studies, however, did not take all her time, and Davis occasionally participated in anti–Vietnam War rallies held outside the U.S. Embassy in Frankfurt.

Davis, however, longed to return home when she read newspaper reports that said the black community in the United States was becoming increasingly radicalized. She later recalled:

> While I was hidden away in West Germany the Black Liberation Movement was undergoing decisive metamorphoses. The slogan "Black Power" sprang out of a march in Mississippi. Organizations were being transfigured— The Student Non-Violent Coordinating Committee [SNCC], a leading civil rights organization, was becoming the foremost advocate of "Black Power." The Congress on Racial Equality [CORE] was undergoing similar transformations. In Newark, [New Jersey], a national Black Power Conference had been organized. In political groups, labor unions, churches and other organizations, Black caucuses were being formed to defend the special interests of Black people. Everywhere there were upheavals. . . . While I was reading philosophy in Frankfurt . . . there were young Black men in Oakland, California, [in the Black Panthers], who had decided that they had to wield arms in order to protect the residents of Oakland's Black community from the indiscriminate police brutality ravaging the area.[77]

Organizing on Campus

In 1967 Davis returned to the United States and enrolled in graduate school at the University of California at San Diego (UCSD). She also began looking for a way to get involved with the Black Power movement. UCSD only had a handful of black students, and Davis began to comb student rosters and even the halls of the dormitories hoping to find enough African Americans to form a black student union. Eventually she found twenty students and workers—about ten showed up at the first meeting, including one black professor from Jamaica.

For her efforts, Davis was soon seen as the black leader on campus. The small black community at UCSD, however, could not satisfy Davis's desire to implement widespread social change. Looking north, she discovered a vibrant—and militant—Black

Power movement gaining strength in the mostly black Watts neighborhood of Los Angeles. Davis soon rented a small apartment in Watts and began attending meetings of several Black Power groups. One, the US-Organization, was led by Ron Karenga, an intellectual equal to Davis, who had graduated from UCLA with a master's in political science. Two other Black Power groups were the United Front and the Black Panthers.

The Los Angeles Black Power groups had conflicting goals and often clashed, at times violently. When Davis first arrived, for example, a gun battle broke out between rival factions at a meeting she attended at the Second Baptist Church in Watts. Davis describes this as a "kick in the teeth" for her idealism, writing:

> [I] discovered that about the only thing we really had in common was skin color. No wonder unity was fragile. . . . There were the cultural . . . organizations, talking about a new culture, a new value system, a new lifestyle among Black people. There were the severely anti-white factions who felt that only the most drastic measure—elimination of all white people—would give Black people the opportunity to live unhampered by racism. Others simply wanted

Davis speaks at a conference at the Communist Party's national headquarters in 1976. Her radical political affiliations had attracted the attention of government intelligence agencies.

to separate and build a distinct Black nation within the United States. And some wanted to return to Africa, the land of our ancestors.[78]

An Outspoken Leader

Of all the political organizations that were forming in Watts, Davis was most attracted to the Black Panther Political Party (BPPP). She temporarily put her graduate studies on the back burner and devoted herself to the organization, which advocated revolution as a way to achieve black equality. Davis's transformation during this period from a shy, retiring student to an outspoken BPPP leader was detailed by Helen Dudar in the *New York Post*, who wrote: "The cool intellectual with the carriage of a duchess, the detached onlooker, became a full participant—a rangy, chain-smoking black woman with a glorious Afro [hairstyle] who ran with the Panthers and signed up with the Communists. . . . "[79]

Dangerous Infighting

Davis had become a symbol of Black Power, but this meant that she faced very real violence in her personal life. In early 1968 an ongoing dispute over the Black Panther name turned violent. Members of an Oakland group, also called the Black Panthers, stormed the offices of the BPPP. Davis was abducted at gunpoint by a drunken Oakland Black Panther who forced her to agree to change her organization's name while he held a gun to her head. Other BPPP members were similarly threatened. To stave off further violence, the BPPP joined forces with the Student Nonviolent Coordinating Committee (SNCC) to form a group called L.A. SNCC. During this merging of the parties, Davis began to associate with black revolutionaries of the era, including Eldridge Cleaver, Stokely Carmichael, H. Rap Brown, and Bobby Seale. Meanwhile Davis, still fearing for her life, bought several guns for self-defense.

Working for L.A. SNCC, Davis was energized, holding rallies to protest police brutality and raising money in urban neighborhoods to defend black leaders such as Huey Newton, who was in jail awaiting trial for allegedly murdering a police officer. Davis also organized youth programs such as the SNCC Youth Corps and the Liberation School, to teach black history and culture as well as revolutionary political philosophy. During this period, the FBI, the CIA, and other government agencies began watching Davis's actions very closely.

Although she was among the best-known black female leaders, Davis, ironically, spent much of her time performing secretarial duties. She often worked in the busy SNCC office, where the phone rang constantly with reports of discrimination and police brutality. Davis and the other two women in the office felt they had a disproportionate share of the workload, as she writes:

> Some of the brothers came around only for staff meetings . . . and whenever we women were involved in something important, they began to talk about "women taking over the organization." . . . All the myths about black women surfaced. [We] were too domineering; we were trying to control everything, including the men—which meant by extension that we wanted to rob them of their manhood. By playing such a leadership role in the organization, some of them insisted, we were aiding and abetting the [white] enemy, who wanted to see black men weak and unable to hold their own. The condemnation was particularly bitter because we were one of the few [black] organizations . . . in Los Angeles, and probably in the country, where women did play a leading role.[80]

Davis faced other problems as well. By the late sixties, SNCC was a major national civil rights organization. Its operating budget was dependent on support from mainstream donors, many of whom were frightened by talk of violent revolution. This led to a disagreement over the curriculum Davis taught in the Liberation School. National leaders wanted young people to learn skills such as radio and TV repair while Davis wanted to teach revolutionary politics and the *Communist Manifesto*. Many felt that this would scare off white liberals who supported SNCC financially. These clashes caused Davis to resign. Soon others followed, and L.A. SNCC was dead.

Becoming a Professor

At this point Davis, who had maintained her commitment to Communist ideals, began to take an active role in the Communist Party itself. In June 1968 she joined the black cell of the party called the Che-Lumumba Club. She also remained committed to completing her education, so shortly thereafter she returned to UCSD where she completed work on her PhD.

With her doctorate in hand, in the autumn of 1969 Davis accepted a position as assistant professor of philosophy at UCLA. By this time, she was an internationally recognized political figure and a symbol of the black liberation movement. This made her appointment very controversial. When the *San Francisco Examiner* ran an article saying that UCLA had hired a "well-qualified

Marxist . . . active in the SDS and Black Panthers,"[81] Davis was fired by the university's board of regents. She sued to be reinstated, and a judge ruled in her favor, saying that the Constitution protects political beliefs and that employees could not be fired, no matter how abhorrent their employers find them. The controversy made Davis a star on campus, and when she appeared for her first class she was greeted by a cheering crowd of two thousand.

The Soledad Brothers

Although she was a popular teacher, Davis continued her political activism within the black community. She had long been a champion of the rights of black prison inmates, and in early 1970, she took up the cause of George L. Jackson, an inmate at Soledad Prison south of San Francisco. The case began in January when a fight broke out among inmates in the exercise yard at Soledad. A guard in the tower started shooting and killed three black men. Three days later, another guard, Vincent Mills, was killed in retaliation by inmates who threw him off a cell block riser to the concrete floor three flights below. Three men, Jackson, a white prisoner named John Cluchette, and a Hispanic man named Fletta Drumgo, were charged with killing Mills. So began the case of the Soledad Brothers.

Jackson had been serving a life sentence for stealing $70 from a gas station. He was, therefore, already a recognized symbol of the

Davis speaks at a rally in Raleigh, North Carolina, in 1974. As a member of the Student Nonviolent Coordinating Committee, Davis organized many such rallies to protest police brutality.

way black men received disproportionate sentences for their crimes. His lawyers and family suggested that he was framed for the murder of the guard because he was a militant who had been teaching revolutionary politics to the other inmates. Davis wrote that the "prison bureaucracy was going to hold [Jackson] symbolically responsible for the spontaneous rebellion [that resulted in the guard's death]."[82]

While all this was happening, the regents were once again trying to fire Davis on the grounds that her political speeches outside the classroom were "unbefitting a university professor."[83] Instead of staying in Los Angeles and fighting for her job, she immersed herself in the cause of exonerating the Soledad Brothers. In the radical tenor of the times, their cause gained instant notoriety, and thousands of people joined in the fight with Davis.

FBI's Ten Most Wanted

During this period, Jackson's seventeen-year-old brother, Jon, became a constant companion to Davis, traveling with her and acting as her bodyguard. On August 7, 1970, Jon Jackson carried out a plan meant to free his brother. He walked into a Marin County courtroom in San Rafael carrying four guns and took over the room. He freed several convicts who were on trial and abducted Judge Harold J. Haley along with the district attorney, Gary Thomas, and three female jurors. Hoping to use the hostages as a bargaining chip to free his brother, Jon tried to escape in a van outside the courtroom. Police officers opened fire, killing Jon, but not before he shot Judge Haley in the head. Thomas was seriously wounded, as was one of the jurors.

A week after the debacle, the Marin County district attorney charged Davis with first-degree murder and kidnapping, alleging that she had purchased three of the four guns used by Jon in the crime. Davis claimed she had purchased the guns for self-protection, and that Jon must have stolen them from her. Davis felt she would never receive a fair trial and abandoned her San Francisco apartment shortly before the police raided it on August 15. She was quickly added to the FBI's "ten most wanted" fugitive list.

Davis managed to elude the FBI for two months before she was arrested in October 1970. Fearing that she was a flight risk, authorities held Davis without bail for sixteen months, much of that time in solitary confinement. The publicity of her case inspired an international "Free Angela Davis" campaign. In 1972 a jury acquitted her of all charges. When her ordeal was over, Davis cofounded the National Alliance Against Racism and Political Repression, which continues its work today.

Today, Angela Davis is a professor at the University of California at Santa Cruz, and she continues to advocate the rights of black prison inmates.

Since that time, Davis has lectured in fifty countries about the racism she feels is inherent in the U.S. criminal justice system. Her articles and essays have appeared in numerous journals, and she is the author of five books. In 2003 Davis taught at the University of California at Santa Cruz and worked in her spare time as an advocate of prison abolition.

In the 1960s Davis was one of the brightest political philosophers of the era. At a time when many other respected college professors avoided confrontation, Davis sacrificed her personal well-being for her beliefs. Although Davis has gained a measure of fame and fortune over the years, she continues to fight for the rights of black prison inmates. This dedication toward those who receive little respect or sympathy from society has allowed Davis to remain true to those values for which she has fought for nearly four decades.

NOTES

Chapter 1: Martin Luther King Jr.

1. Stephen B. Oates, *Let the Trumpet Sound: The Life of Martin Luther King, Jr.* New York: Harper & Row, 1982, pp. 3–4.

2. Martin Luther King Jr., *The Autobiography of Martin Luther King, Jr.*, ed. Clayborne Carson. New York: Warner Books, 1998, p. 7.

3. Oates, *Let the Trumpet Sound*, p. 32.

4. Quoted in James A. Colaiaco, *Martin Luther King, Jr.: Apostle of Militant Nonviolence.* New York: St. Martin's, 1988, p. 9.

5. Lerone Bennett Jr., *What Manner of Man: A Biography of Martin Luther King, Jr.* Chicago: Johnson, 1968, p. 71.

6. Quoted in Colaiaco, *Martin Luther King, Jr.*, pp. 90–91.

Chapter 2: Dagmar Wilson

7. Quoted in Amy Swerdlow, *Women Strike for Peace.* Chicago: University of Chicago Press, 1993, p. 54.

8. Quoted in Otto Nathan and Heinz Norden, *Einstein on Peace.* New York: Simon & Schuster, 1960, pp. 640–41.

9. Dagmar Wilson, *Journal of Women Strike for Peace: Commemorating Eighteen Years of Conscientious Concerns for the Future of the World's Children.* New York: Women Strike for Peace, 1979, p. 2.

10. Quoted in Swerdlow, *Women Strike for Peace*, p. 18.

11. Quoted in Swerdlow, *Women Strike for Peace*, p. 15.

12. Swerdlow, *Women Strike for Peace*, p. 16.

13. Quoted in Swerdlow, *Women Strike for Peace*, p. 15.

14. Quoted in C.P. Trussell, "House Sets Study of Peace Groups: Walter Cites Allegations of Communist Infiltration." *New York Times*, December 7, 1962, p. 3.

15. Quoted in Swerdlow, *Women Strike for Peace*, pp. 116–17.

16. Quoted in Swerdlow, *Women Strike for Peace*, p. 117.

17. Quoted in Blanche Linden-Ward and Carol Hurd Green, *American Women in the 1960s: Changing the Future.* New York: Twayne, 1993, pp. 165–66.

18. Quoted in Berkeley Arts Center Association, *The Whole World Is Watching*. Berkeley, CA: Berkeley Arts Center Association, 2001.

19. Quoted in Edith Villastrigo, "Women Strike for Peace," Comprehensive Test Ban Treaty, September 24, 1996. http://prop1.org.

Chapter 3: Tom Hayden

20. Quoted in Tom Hayden, *Reunion: A Memoir*. New York: Random House, 1988, p. 13.

21. Hayden, *Reunion*, p. 61.

22. Hayden, *Reunion*, pp. 39–40.

23. Quoted in Zeitgeist Films, "A History of the Students for a Democratic Society (SDS)," 2003. www.zeitgeistfilms.com.

24. Hayden, *Reunion*, pp. 175–76.

25. Quoted in Clark Dougan and Samuel Lipsman, eds. *A Nation Divided*, Boston: Boston, 1984, p. 104.

26. Hayden, *Reunion*, p. 275.

27. Tom Hayden, "Two, Three, Many Columbias," *Ramparts*, June 15, 1968.

28. Terry H. Anderson, *The Movement and the Sixties*. New York: Oxford University Press, 1995, p. 221.

29. Hayden, *Reunion*, pp. 302–303.

30. Hayden, *Reunion*, p. 319.

31. Quoted in Hayden, *Reunion*, p. 339.

32. Hayden, *Reunion*, p. 446.

33. Tree Media Group, "Roundtables." www.treemedia.com.

Chapter 4: Cesar Chavez

34. Quoted in Susan Ferris and Ricardo Sandoval, *The Fight in the Fields: Cesar Chavez and the Farmworkers Movement*. New York: Harcourt Brace, 1997, p. 13.

35. Quoted in Jacques E. Levy, *Cesar Chavez: Autobiography of La Causa*. New York: W.W. Norton, 1975, pp. 74–75.

36. Quoted in Levy, *Cesar Chavez*, pp. 35–36.

37. Richard Griswold del Castillo and Richard A. Garcia, *César Chavez: A Triumph of Spirit*. Norman: University of Oklahoma Press, 1995, pp. 23–24.

38. Quoted in Levy, *Cesar Chavez*, p. 103.

39. Quoted in Levy, *Cesar Chavez*, p. 151.

40. Quoted in Ferris and Sandoval, *The Fight in the Fields*, p. 89.

41. Quoted in Levy, *Cesar Chavez*, pp. 272–73.

Chapter 5: Betty Friedan

42. Betty Friedan, *Life So Far*. New York: Simon & Schuster, 2000, p. 26.

43. Quoted in Judith Hennessee, *Betty Friedan: Her Life*. New York: Random House, 1999, p. 14.

44. Quoted in Janann Sherman, ed., *Interviews with Betty Friedan*. Jackson: University Press of Mississippi, 2002, p. 13.

45. Quoted in Friedan, *Life So Far*, p. 62.

46. Friedan, *Life So Far*, p. 79.

47. Quoted in Friedan, *Life So Far*, p. 101.

48. Friedan, *Life So Far*, p. 104.

49. Quoted in Friedan, *Life So Far*, p. 103.

50. Quoted in Barry G. Cole, *Television*. New York: Free Press, 1970, p. 268.

51. Quoted in Friedan, *Life So Far*, pp. 167–68.

52. Quoted in Sherman, *Interviews with Betty Friedan*, p. 19.

53. Quoted in Friedan, *Life So Far*, p. 219.

54. Friedan, *Life So Far*, p. 221.

55. Friedan, *Life So Far*, pp. 232–33.

56. Hennessee, *Betty Friedan*, p. 140.

57. Quoted in Irwin Unger and Debi Unger, eds., *The Times Were a Changin'*. New York: Three Rivers Press, 1998, p. 203.

Chapter 6: Abbie Hoffman

58. Jonah Raskin, *For the Hell of It: The Life and Times of Abbie Hoffman*. Berkeley: University of California Press, 1996, p. xxii.

59. Quoted in Raskin, *For the Hell of It*, p. 5.

60. Raskin, *For the Hell of It*, p. 13.

61. Abbie Hoffman, *The Autobiography of Abbie Hoffman*. New York: Four Walls Eight Windows, 2000, p. 24.

62. Hoffman, *The Autobiography of Abbie Hoffman*, p. 40.

63. Hoffman, *The Autobiography of Abbie Hoffman*, p. 41.

64. Quoted in Larry Sloman, *Steal This Dream*. New York: Doubleday, 1998, p. 24.

65. Jack Hoffman and Daniel Simon, *Run Run Run: The Lives of Abbie Hoffman*. New York: G.P. Putnam's Sons, 1994, p. 71.

66. Hoffman, *The Autobiography of Abbie Hoffman*, p. 86.

67. Quoted in Raskin, *For the Hell of It*, p. 101.

68. Quoted in Abbie Hoffman, *The Best of Abbie Hoffman*. New York: Four Walls Eight Windows, 1989, p. 52.

69. Abbie Hoffman, *Soon to Be a Major Motion Picture*. New York: Perigee Books, 1980, pp. 144–45.

70. Clark Dougan and Samuel Lipsman, eds., *A Nation Divided*. Boston: Boston, 1984 p. 128.

71. Hoffman, *The Autobiography of Abbie Hoffman*, p. 187.

Chapter 7: Angela Davis

72. Marc Olden, *Angela Davis*. New York: Lancer Books, 1973, p. 56.

73. Angela Davis, *Angela Davis: An Autobiography*. New York: Random House, 1974, pp. 79–80.

74. Davis, *Angela Davis*, p. 111.

75. Quoted in Olden, *Angela Davis*, p. 64.

76. Quoted in Olden, *Angela Davis*, p. 73.

77. Davis, *Angela Davis*, p. 144.

78. Davis, *Angela Davis*, p. 159.

79. Quoted in J.A. Parker, *Angela Davis: The Making of a Revolutionary*. New Rochelle, NY: Arlington House, 1973, p. 93.

80. Davis, *Angela Davis*, p. 181.

81. Quoted in The Professor, *Angela*. North Hollywood, CA: Leisure Books, 1971, p. 106.

82. Davis, *Angela Davis*, p. 253.

83. Quoted in Davis, *Angela Davis*, p. 273.

John H. Bunzel, *New Force on the Left*. Stanford, CA: Hoover Institution Press, 1983. A biography of Tom Hayden that focuses on his work after the Vietnam War ended as he campaigned for increased honesty and integrity in corporate America.

Lucile Davis, *Cesar Chavez: A Photo-Illustrated Biography*. Mankato, MN: Bridgestone Books, 1998. Presents the life story of the Mexican American labor leader who achieved justice for migrant farmworkers by creating a union to protect their rights.

Abbie Hoffman, *The Best of Abbie Hoffman*. New York: Four Walls Eight Windows, 1989. A compilation of Yippies founder Abbie Hoffman's best writing over the years, including excerpts from his groundbreaking books *Revolution for the Hell of It*, *Woodstock Nation*, and *Steal This Book*. Also included are newer articles written in the 1980s.

Sally Senzell Isaacs, *America in the Time of Martin Luther King, Jr.: 1948 to 1976*. Des Plaines, IL: Heinemann Library, 2000. The story of racial conflict and resolution in the United States after World War II, with King's role in solving problems nonviolently.

Coretta Scott King, *My Life with Martin Luther King, Jr.* New York: Holt, Rinehart and Winston, 1969. An inside look at the life and work of the noted civil rights leader, from the viewpoint of his wife.

Martin Luther King Jr., *Letter from the Birmingham Jail*. San Francisco: HarperSanFrancisco, 1994. An eloquent and forceful letter against social injustice written in April 1963 while King was in jail for participating in civil rights demonstrations.

Susan Taylor-Boyd, *Betty Friedan: Voice for Women's Rights, Advocate of Human Rights*. Milwaukee, WI: G. Stevens Children's Books, 1990. Follows the life and work of the feminist who wrote *The Feminine Mystique* and helped found the National Organization for Women.

Michael V. Uschan, *Martin Luther King Jr.* San Diego: Lucent Books, 2003. The life story of one of the twentieth century's most inspiring and influential figures, a man who utilized tactics of nonviolence to fight racism and win new freedoms for African Americans.

WORKS CONSULTED

Books

Terry H. Anderson, *The Movement and the Sixties*. New York: Oxford University Press, 1995. A book that details the historic social movements of the 1960s from civil rights sit-ins to the antiwar marches to the women's liberation movement. The book explores the struggle for equality for African Americans, Native Americans, women, Chicanos, and others.

Philip D. Beidler, *Scriptures for a Generation: What We Were Reading in the 1960s*. Athens, GA: University of Georgia Press, 1994. A scholarly work that explores how best-selling books of the sixties examined war, racism, sexism, and other important issues.

Lerone Bennett Jr., *What Manner of Man: A Biography of Martin Luther King, Jr.* Chicago: Johnson, 1968. A biography of the great civil rights leader written in the months after his assassination.

Berkeley Arts Center Association, *The Whole World Is Watching*. Berkeley, CA: Berkeley Arts Center Association, 2001. A book of photos portraying various aspects of the 1960s and '70s peace and justice movements, with essays by a number of eyewitnesses to events associated with those movements.

Stewart Burns, *Social Movements of the 1960s*. Boston: Twayne, 1990. One of the volumes in the Social Movements series, it covers the rise of the antiwar, the civil rights, and the women's liberation movements, and their long-ranging influences on Western society and culture.

James A. Colaiaco, *Martin Luther King, Jr.: Apostle of Militant Nonviolence*. New York: St. Martin's, 1988. Covers the work of Dr. King, focusing on his unshakable faith in nonviolent resistance from the time of the Montgomery bus boycott until his death in 1968.

Barry G. Cole, *Television*. New York: The Free Press, 1970. Reprints of articles that appeared in *T.V. Guide* magazine in the 1960s. Topics include the quality of news, political coverage, programming, advertising, minorities on screen, censorship, and the effects of television on society.

Bettye Collier-Thomas and V.P. Franklin, eds., *Sisters in the Struggle*. New York: New York University Press, 2001. A collection of sixteen essays by African American women who actively participated in the civil rights and the Black Power movements.

Angela Davis, *Angela Davis: An Autobiography*. New York: Random House, 1974. The life story of a woman who was a Black Panther, a Communist, a fugitive, and a college professor.

Clark Dougan and Samuel Lipsman, eds., *A Nation Divided*. Boston: Boston, 1984. One of the books in the Vietnam Experience series, this edition explores events in the United States during the time of the Vietnam War, including the protest movement, those who opposed the protesters, and media perspectives.

Betty Friedan, *The Feminine Mystique*. New York: Norton, 1963. The groundbreaking book about the lives of suburban women in the early sixties and the unhappiness faced by many because of gender discrimination.

———, *It Changed My Life*. New York: Random House, 1976. Excerpts of the most famous speeches and articles written by a leading women's rights activist and founding member of the National Organization for Women.

———, *Life So Far*. New York: Simon & Schuster, 2000. The autobiography of the woman who founded the modern feminist movement in the 1960s.

Richard Griswold del Castillio and Richard A. Garcia, *César Chavez: A Triumph of Spirit*. Norman: University of Oklahoma Press, 1995. An illuminating biography of the leader of the farmworkers movement.

Tom Hayden, *Reunion: A Memoir*. New York: Random House, 1988. An autobiography by a man who was one of the founding members of SDS, led dozens of protests in the sixties, and was put on trial for conspiracy after the Chicago Democratic Convention. Hayden later went on to marry actress Jane Fonda and served many years as a state assemblyman and state senator in California.

———, *Trial*. New York: Holt, Rinehart and Winston, 1970. A recounting of the Chicago Seven trial in which the author was tried with six others for conspiracy to incite a riot and other felony charges.

———, "Two, Three, Many Columbias," *Ramparts*, June 15, 1968. An article about the goals of the students who instigated the Columbia College takeover in April 1968.

Judith Hennessee, *Betty Friedan: Her Life*. New York: Random House, 1999. An insightful biography that analyzes the life and career of one of the founding members of the National Organization for Women.

Abbie Hoffman, *The Autobiography of Abbie Hoffman*. New York: Four Walls Eight Windows, 2000. Originally published in 1980, the author tells the story of his life with the outrageous humor and stunning candor that made him a public figure in the 1960s.

———, *Soon to Be a Major Motion Picture*. New York: Perigee Books, 1980. The autobiography of Abbie Hoffman detailing his childhood in Massachusetts and his elevation to a national leader as founder of the Yippies.

Jack Hoffman and Daniel Simon, *Run Run Run: The Lives of Abbie Hoffman*. New York: G.P. Putnam's Sons, 1994. The detailed story of America's most famous modern revolutionary written by his brother.

Martin Luther King Jr. *The Autobiography of Martin Luther King, Jr.*, ed. Clayborne Carson. New York: Warner Books, 1998. A chronicle of the life and times of one of history's most revered political activists, woven together from thousands of recordings, speeches, letters, and other documents.

Blanche Linden-Ward and Carol Hurd Green, *American Women in the 1960s: Changing the Future*. New York: Twayne, 1993. A comprehensive book detailing women's roles in the culture of the 1960s in such fields as the civil rights movement, higher education, media, and the arts.

Otto Nathan and Heinz Norden, *Einstein on Peace*. New York: Simon & Schuster, 1960. Statements on peace by the renowned physicist whose theories were used by others to create atomic weapons.

Stephen B. Oates, *Let the Trumpet Sound: The Life of Martin Luther King, Jr.* New York: Harper & Row, 1982. A comprehensive and compelling biography of King based on intensive research.

Marc Olden, *Angela Davis*. New York: Lancer Books, 1973. A book about Angela Davis and her impact as a leader upon the black community.

J.A. Parker, *Angela Davis: The Making of a Revolutionary*. New Rochelle, NY: Arlington House, 1973. A biography of the sixties revolutionary with an emphasis on the life experiences that drove her political activism.

The Professor, *Angela*. North Hollywood, CA: Leisure Books, 1971. An anonymous biography of Angela Davis written at a time when she was on the list of the FBI's most wanted criminals.

Jonah Raskin, *For the Hell of It: The Life and Times of Abbie Hoffman*. Berkeley: University of California Press, 1996. A compelling biography about the triumphs, despairs, and follies in the life of the Yippies founder.

Janann Sherman, ed., *Interviews with Betty Friedan*. Jackson: University Press of Mississippi, 2002. A collection of interviews with the founder of the women's liberation movement, taken from magazine articles and television stories.

Larry Sloman, *Steal This Dream*. New York: Doubleday, 1998. An oral biography of Abbie Hoffman taken from quotes from friends, family, fellow Yippies, and various articles and documents.

Amy Swerdlow, *Women Strike for Peace*. Chicago: University of Chicago Press, 1993. The historical account of the Women Strike for Peace movement by a founding member of the organization that brought together the peace and feminist movements in the early sixties.

Irwin Unger and Debi Unger, eds., *The Times Were a Changin'*. New York: Three Rivers Press, 1998. An anthology of "speeches, manifestos, court decisions, and groundbreaking journalism of the Sixties," with excerpts from documents concerning the antiwar movement, women's liberation, the race to the moon, and other compelling subjects.

Dagmar Wilson, *Journal of Women Strike for Peace: Commemorating Eighteen Years of Conscientious Concerns for the Future of the World's Children*. New York: Women Strike for Peace, 1979. The story of the WSP, its famous strike in 1961, its work against the Vietnam War, and the organization's protests against nuclear testing in the 1970s.

Internet Sources

Sonia Pressman Fuentes, "Sex Maniac," Feminism/Women in Philosophy, 1999. www.erraticimpact.com/~feminism/html/sonia_pressman_fuentes2.htm. Excerpts from the chapter "Sex Maniac" in Fuentes's book, *Eat First—You Don't Know What They'll Give You: The Adventures of an Immigrant Family and Their Feminist Daughter*. The author was the first female lawyer hired by the Equal Employment Opportunity Commission in the midsixties.

Tree Media Group, "Roundtables." www.treemedia.com/roundtables/roundtable03.htm. Contains biographies of several activists, including Tom Hayden.

Edith Villastrigo, "Women Strike for Peace," Comprehensive Test Ban Treaty, September 24, 1996. http://prop1.org/2000/ctbtwsp.htm. States the goals of the WSP organization.

Zeitgeist Films, "A History of the Students for a Democratic Society (SDS)," 2003. www.zeitgeistfilms.com/current/rebels/rebels.history.html. A review of a documentary film about SDS, with information about the history of the organization.

PICTURE CREDITS

ABOUT THE AUTHOR

Stuart A. Kallen is the author of more than 160 nonfiction books for children and young adults. He has written on topics ranging from the theory of relativity to the history of rock and roll. In addition, Mr. Kallen has written award-winning children's videos and television scripts. In his spare time, Stuart A. Kallen is a singer/songwriter/guitarist in San Diego.